Ecotourism

A Practical Guide for Rural Communities

Ecotourism

A Practical Guide for Rural Communities

Sue Beeton

LANDLINKS PRESS

National Library of Australia
Cataloguing-in-Publication entry

Beeton, Sue
Ecotourism: A Practical Guide for Rural Communities
Bibliography.
ISBN 0 643 06359 5.

1. Ecotourism – Australia
2. Rural development – Australia
I. Title.

338.4791

LANDLINKS PRESS
PO Box 1139
Collingwood 3066
Australia

Tel: (03) 9662 7666 Int: +61 3 9662 7666
Fax: (03) 9662 7555 Int: +61 3 9662 7555

Foreword

Australians have always felt an almost romantic attachment to the bush. Whether real or imaginary, urban dwellers happily connect to popular images from 'the wide brown land'.

Important as they are, there is a great deal more to the Australian bush than kangaroos and koalas. Gradually we are all being exposed to non-consumptive and educative pursuits in rural Australia which come wrapped in the tag of ecotourism.

For struggling towns and regions of the bush, this term should be a signal spelling 'opportunity'. Ecotourism can provide investment and jobs which actively encourage environmental understanding, appreciation and conservation. Sue Beeton has succeeded in putting together a much-needed and most comprehensive reference for individuals and communities already involved and wanting to get into ecotourism.

We have all seen the problems created where industries have emerged without guidelines and standards. For ecotourism to continue to flourish with widespread acceptance of its sustainability and ethics, the industry must aspire to the highest level of excellence. This book will help all those involved in ecotourism reach that level.

Kerry Lonergan
Executive Producer
ABC 'Landline'

Acknowledgments

As with any publication there are many people and organisations that assist in bringing it together, and this is no exception. Kathy Shackleton deserves a very special mention as the person who first suggested that I may be able to write "something on ecotourism for rural people", starting me on this fascinating journey. I would also like to recognise two other associates (and friends), Tess Sampson and Fran Carew, who have given me exceptional support over the years, encouraging my first publication and giving me the confidence to "soldier on".

All the ecotourism operators who freely provided me with information for the case studies and examples, often with very short notice, have impressed me with their willingness to cooperate and share their experiences, and my appreciation goes out to you all, even those who did not actually make it into the book — there are so many people becoming aware of the environment that it is heartening that there were more examples than I could use!

Recognition must also go to the Ecotourism Tourism Association of Australia who not only provided numerous case studies through their informative newsletter but also through their annual Ecotourism Conference, which provided the opportunity to meet and discuss many of the issues considered in this book with the leaders of the Australian ecotourism industry.

And thanks to my students who have been the first to see much of this work and provided me with direct and indirect feedback on the effectiveness of my style and the information provided.

This publication also provides me with the opportunity to publicly thank my parents who have supported and encouraged me in my work in the tourism industry over the past ten years – it has been said before, but without such support I would not be writing this acknowledgment today.

Contents

Introduction

Unemployment is a major social and economic issue in Australia and New Zealand, particularly for young people in rural areas. Many families have seen their children leave the country for employment and opportunities offered in the city. This flow must be reduced, otherwise we will have no people to provide the goods and services that we all rely on to survive.

Diversification of rural industry appears to be the key to survival in today's economic and social climate. Tourism, particularly in country areas, can work extremely well as a companion industry to existing rural businesses by, for example, providing accommodation and "farm-stays" on a working property. However, if you decide to diversify into tourism, you need to make sure that the enterprises do not conflict, such as at harvesting times, when everyone needs to be out in the paddock, not looking after tourists. By considering these elements in your business plan and introducing some simple systems and controls for each activity, such problems can be avoided. This issue is covered in Chapter 6.

Tourism, and particularly ecotourism, with its focus on natural resources, has the potential to generate a wide range of jobs for young people in remote and rural communities, enabling them to remain in the country. It is one of the fastest growing industries in Australia and New Zealand, overtaking traditional exports such as coal, meat and wool (all rural-based commodities) as Australia's largest export earner. Recent estimates from the World Travel and Tourism Commission show that travel and tourism generate the equivalent of one million jobs in Australia and 200,000 in New Zealand — this is obviously an area that needs to be treated seriously.

So, what is a "tourism product"? Broadly speaking, it is anything that can be offered to people for their interest, purchase, use, or consumption that may satisfy a need. It can include actual objects, services, places, people, organisations and ideas. This definition covers just about anything you can think of, as tourism can relate to everything we do. Although you may think your day-to-day work would not interest anyone else, somewhere out there a group of people is very likely fascinated by road-building, fencing, selling rural produce, fruit growing or wheat production. The same is true for the environment — the natural assets that we take for granted are often major reasons for a person to visit our area.

Chapters 1 and 2 look at what ecotourism is, the special characteristics of ecotourists, and explains the connection between the environment and tourism generally, as well as in ecotourism.

Most tourism is really just "showing off" things that are already there, and in the case of ecotourism this is your own natural, local environment. For example, your property may be near a significant natural site or environment such as a National Park, World Heritage Area, Conservation Zone or an unusual natural phenomenon. You may even have significant natural attractions on your own property, such as wildlife, landscape, native bushland, spectacular views, beautiful river sites or heritage areas. Even land that has been degraded through inappropriate farming, mining, logging or natural causes, and is being restored can be a "natural attraction", particularly if it is part of a local Land Care program. This case is considered in Chapter 4,

The next step, examined in Chapter 5, is "Working with the Environment". This section includes information on building design and environmental regulations, which can be used in any aspect of your business, be it tourism, ecotourism or farming. So, are you suited to running a tourism business? Chapter 6 examines the personal attributes needed by a tourism operator, in particular communication, people and hosting skills. If you are not comfortable with people and disruption to your work and home routines, you may need to reconsider your decision to get into tourism, which is a highly personalised "people business". One solution could be to employ skilled staff or go into partnership with someone whose skills suitably complement yours.

Unplanned tourism growth can create as many problems as it solves, and one of the aims of this book is to assist you in planning and developing your tourism venture (be it "eco" or any other type) so that the benefits can be achieved. Also, just as with farming where crops or stock would not be introduced without the right conditions, similarly ecotourism cannot be introduced where the environment is not able to sustain it, or where the impact on the local community would clearly be adverse, or there is insufficient interest in the product.

For example, while ecotourism will create employment, if the community does not have the appropriate skills they either have to learn them or import other people to do the work. Bringing new people in may encourage a growth in support industries to service their needs, but may also displace the local population, creating more problems than before. Chapter 3 considers such positive and negative social impacts, emphasising the importance of both indigenous and non-indigenous community involvement in tourism.

On a more positive note, Australia leads the world in many ecotourism areas, such as industry accreditation (a world first, discussed in Chapter 6), training and government commitment, at local, regional, state and federal levels.

Of course, even if your ecotourism venture is environmentally and socially sustainable, it must also be economically sustainable. The "bottom line" is covered in Chapter 7.

This book is intended to provide an overall understanding of ecotourism and the broader tourism industry. As such it includes many Australian and New Zealand case studies and examples of operators who are achieving in different areas. The book has been written with the rural person in mind, and with its theoretical elements built firmly on a practical basis it should also be of interest to students of tourism and the environment.

The contact details in Appendix Three are as up-to-date as possible, and provide both the operator and student with extensive sources of further information. Many of the organisations have been contacted during the course of researching and writing this book and have been extremely helpful in providing information, much of which is listed in the References. This section provides suggestions for further reading with some comments about the extent to which each reference was used in this publication and the degree of additional information it may provide.

For many of you this will be the beginning of a journey that I hope will take you further than you thought possible!

| What is Ecotourism?

Introduction

The term "ecotourism" has already been referred to a few times, but what does it mean? The term was first used by Hector Ceballos-Lascurain in Mexico in 1988, and since then much heated debate has occurred about what it should mean and how it is actually being used by tourism operators. Some tourism operators use the word "ecotourism" purely as a marketing and advertising tool without offering their customers any type of environmental experience. The debate, which will probably continue in academic circles for ever, makes a great essay topic for students. However, there is some general agreement on the elements of ecotourism, of which there are three main ones:

1 Ecotourism is nature-based (occurs in a natural setting)
2 It is educative
3 It is managed in a sustainable manner

These elements will be examined in more detail in later chapters, but a brief overview is provided here to introduce these important concepts.

1 Nature-Based

This is the "eco" (ecological, not economic) element of ecotourism, and is really self-explanatory. Without some reference to nature and the environment, a tourism operation could not be considered ecological. "Nature-based" refers to both the flora and fauna of an area, and can be associated with environments that have been modified by man. For example, on a farm where parts of the land are being restored to some form of "natural environment", by for example, restoring eroded river banks, this work could be regarded as nature-based. While the main reason for the work may be economic and agricultural, the attendant environmental benefits could become part of an ecotourism product.

Not all nature-based tourism is regarded as ecotourism — it must also include the other two elements, education and sustainability.

2 Education and Interpretation

With the increased interest in (and number of) nature-based documentaries on television and in other parts of the media, as well as a shift in education towards the environment, many people are becoming more socially and environmentally aware. As tourists travel more widely, they are becoming more adventurous and more questioning about what they see. Many people want tourism experiences where they are provided with information that helps them to understand the places they visit.

It is no longer possible to ferry tourists around in a bus, with a few obligatory photo stops, without providing other information. They are interested in what they see and want to know more, not only about the natural environment, but also about indigenous heritage and cultural aspects of the region. Ecotourism plays a particular role in this area, with the provision of information and other learning opportunities being integral to the product, not an afterthought.

However, this educational component must still be provided in an interesting manner — after all, the ecotourist is on a holiday. Many operators include personal knowledge, employ specialists as required (such as botanists, biologists etc) and carry a good reference library that they and their guests can use.

3 Sustainable Management

All tourism, not just ecotourism, should be handled in an environmentally sustainable manner. Apart from considerations about our responsibility towards the future of the planet, we are responsible for the future of our tourism businesses — if we destroy the natural attractions and environment that people came to experience, they will go elsewhere.

Sustainable management means managing the physical stresses on the environment, such as the number of people and the way they behave, by introducing minimal impact techniques of waste disposal and minimisation, and minimisation of energy use. Issues related to souveniring items and interfering with wildlife are also part of sustainable management. Some tourism operators have developed creative solutions to resolve some of these difficult problems and this area is covered in some detail in Chapters 4 and 5.

However, sustainability refers not only to the natural environment. Those involved in ecotourism recognise the need for local communities to benefit from tourism, and the aim to sustain the well-being (both culturally and financially) of local people is an important aspect of the ecotourism philosophy. This can be achieved by purchasing goods and services locally and employing as many local staff as possible, as well as through personal financial and time commitments. For example, an ecotourism operator may be on the local tourism association board, chamber of commerce, scout group, land care group, or provide money or physical services to conservation and other community projects.

Practising What They Preach

Award-winning New Zealand ecotourism operator, Catlins Wildlife Trackers Ecotours, takes its conservation commitments seriously. While on tours, guides make wildlife observations, trap predators and remove weeds. They also run a series of workshops that focus on practical ways to assist in a specific area, such as rare plant restoration and conservation, and penguin conservation. These are working holidays where guests provide their services to specific programs on a voluntary basis. By offering practical assistance the company is able to support local conservation programs in a way that is also interesting to their clients.

As well as commercial ecotour operators, volunteer environmental groups such as the Australian and New Zealand Scientific Exploration Society, the Australian Trust for Conservation Volunteers, and Earthwatch, also run scientific expeditions. Their contact details are in Appendix Three.

A relatively simple definition of ecotourism that covers all the aspects outlined above has been adopted by the Ecotourism Association of Australia:

"Ecotourism is ecologically sustainable tourism that fosters environmental and cultural understanding, appreciation and conservation."

Many academic papers look at other definitions and complexities. If you are interested in more information on the search for a definition of ecotourism, some papers are listed in the References.

While researching the tourism industry, you will come across references to other types of tourism, such as rural tourism, nature-based tourism, farm tourism, adventure tourism, industrial tourism, indigenous tourism, cultural tourism and so on. It can be confusing working out where ecotourism fits in to the picture, but basically it is part of the broader rural or nature-based tourism industry. Also included in the rural and nature-based area would be farm tourism and adventure tourism (and possibly indigenous tourism), elements of which can be incorporated into ecotourism. The main difference between ecotourism and other types of tourism that are based in the natural environment is the educational aspect and its associated ethical stand of supporting and encouraging ongoing conservation and direct benefits to the local community.

So, if you are thinking about starting any other type of tourism enterprise (such as adventure or farmstay) this book will still be useful as many of the areas covered here will be relevant and transferable to your enterprise. The concept of ecological sustainability is not just for ecotourism — all tourism must be sustainable, both ecologically, socially and economically.

How Big is Ecotourism?

As part of the overall tourism industry, ecotourism is regarded as a niche enterprise that caters for particular interests of certain tourists. It has only been recognised as a separate form of tourism for the past ten years, so it is certainly not as old as, say, cultural tours of Europe. Although it is still relatively small in numbers, it shows a higher rate of growth than any other tourism niche market.

The emergence of a "conservation ethic" in most western societies has encouraged the development and growth of ecotourism. Although statistics on ecotourism are not easy to obtain, the World Tourism Organisation predicts that by 2000 most of the increase in worldwide tourism will come from active, nature and culture-related travel, while other reports indicate a 25–30 per cent growth in nature-based tourism (with tourism in general growing at around 7–8 per cent). In Australia the number of international visitors from 1989 to 1994 undertaking a bushwalk increased by 60 per cent, and the number who went on a safari tour increased by 70 per cent. Although this growth comes from a relatively small base, it certainly indicates a fantastic potential.

In 1995 Australia had 600 identified ecotourism operators, employing the equivalent of 4,500 full-time staff. These businesses had a combined annual turnover of $250 million, and their growth is expected to double by 2000.

Types of Ecotourism Development

Regardless of where or how they are travelling, tourists need to be accommodated, whether it be in commercial accommodation or with friends and relatives (known as VFR — visiting friends and relatives). An enormous range of tourist accommodation can be incorporated into an ecotourism product:

- eco-resorts (medium to large scale)
- purpose-built campsites, both permanent and semi-permanent
- caravan parks
- bed and breakfast (B&Bs)
- lodge/backpacker hostels
- guest houses
- farmstays
- huts/cabins
- marinas
- house boats

- yachts
- cruising vessels

As well as utilising existing natural resources such as those found in national parks, ecotourism projects can also create attractions, such as:

- sanctuaries (can be privately as well as publicly owned and managed)
- aquariums and zoos (not all these are "eco")
- education, information and interpretation centres
- outdoor museums providing natural as well as cultural heritage

Considerable infrastructure may be required to run an ecotour, such as:

- boardwalks
- look-outs
- hardened pathways, steps
- barbeque and picnic facilities
- pontoons/anchor points
- restaurants and cafes
- signage
- interpretation centres
- toilet facilities
- car parking facilities

Local councils and land management agencies provide much of this infrastructure, particularly in national parks, but it is something that needs to be considered when planning tours, particularly if you are using privately owned land.

Chapter 5 covers the concepts of environmental design, building and development.

Range of Ecotourism Activities

Ecotourism includes many activities that are common to other forms of tourism. They are differentiated by the underlying philosophy and education components. For example, photography could be part of any tourism activity (and usually is), but when it is combined with information on what is being photographed and opportunities to experience the environment it becomes an ecotour activity.

Other ecotourism activities could include sightseeing, bushwalking, camping, wild flower viewing, bird watching, wildlife viewing, night walks, special interest scientific tours (for botanists, ornithologists, geographers, historians etc), and adventure based tours such as cross-country skiing, white water rafting, and mountaineering.

Even if a tourist only spends part of their holiday on an ecotourism activity (say one or two days), they are still considered as "ecotourists" because they have undertaken that activity and shown an interest in the ethics and concepts

5

of ecotourism. They are often referred to as "soft ecotourists", whereas a tourist spending most of their trip on ecotourism activities is considered to be a "hard ecotourist".

Ecotourism: Many Different Activities

Catlins Wildlife Trackers Ecotours offers a wide range of activities, including:

- Observing and learning about New Zealand sea lions and fur seals
- Observing and learning about yellow eyed and little blue penguins
- Observing and learning about sea birds, such as gulls, terns, shags, and sooty shearwaters
- Observing and learning about wader birds, such as oyster catchers, stilts, herons, godwits, and royal spoonbills
- Observing and learning about forest birds, such as bellbirds, fantails, tomtits, tuis, and wood pigeons ...
- Observing and learning about rare or seldom seen birds, such as yellow heads, fern birds, and kingfishers
- Observing and learning about spiders, wetas, glow worms and other creatures
- Star gazing, and learning about the southern sky
- Beach walking, looking at and learning about seaweeds and shells
- Walking the cliff tops, and learning about the formation of the land
- Forest walking, and learning about NZ native forests, beech and podocarp
- Visiting and learning about early Maori historic sites
- Visiting and learning about early European settlement sites, the old railway, the railway tunnel, and historic sawmilling relics
- Visiting waterfalls
- Visiting Lake Wilkie and learning about the development of podocarp forest
- Visiting caves of various sizes
- Fossil finding and geologising
- Learning about the river environment while boating, kayaking or snorkelling
- Swimming and body surfing
- Learning about the marine environment and kelp forests while snorkelling
- Exploring rock pools and the intertidal zone
- Reading, from our extensive library with its emphasis on natural history and local history
- Contributing to conservation by collecting litter, keeping observation records, protecting rare plants
- Eating, drinking and talking
- Watching the sun rise
- Walking on the moonlit beach
- Observing Hectors dolphins
- Observing elephant seals
- Observing albatross at sea
- Climbing hills
- Playing with lego or Cloudberry, the sausage dog
- Relaxing

From Catlins WWW site (http://www.es.co.nz/~catlinw/home.htm)

Benefits for Local Communities

Ecotourism has the potential to increase the value of tourism to the local economy. At the same time, it can improve the experience of visitors and provide a positive force to assist in the conservation of resources and local communities, both indigenous and non-indigenous.

Economic Benefits

Tourism in general, and ecotourism in particular, can diversify and increase the rate base of a community by encouraging new businesses to establish, and by bringing people into the area. This injects new money from outside the region into the local economy, and flows through to the residents in terms of increased employment, new business opportunities, better educational and recreational facilities, residential development and cultural opportunities.

The National Ecotourism Strategy released in 1994 by the Commonwealth Department of Tourism identified the following economic benefits attributable to ecotourism:

- growth of employment in the area
- distribution of income directly to regional and local communities via goods and services
- tendency of greater length of stay by ecotourists as compared with tourists generally
- local infrastructure development
- generation of income for conservation and public land management through permit fees
- additional foreign exchange earnings

1 Growth of Employment in the Area

An estimated 55 jobs are created for every 1000 additional international tourists, and a similar ratio would apply for domestic tourists. According to the Australian Conservation Foundation, ecotourism employment has increased by 131 per cent since 1988, most of it in local regional areas, working in small service businesses and product suppliers (retail shops, service stations, hotels, motels, bed & breakfasts, tour operators and guides).

Although many ecotourism operators are small, family-based businesses employing a limited number of full-time staff, they provide employment indirectly by purchasing goods and services locally.

With most ecotour operators utilising publicly-owned land and infrastructure such as national parks, state forests, parks service information and interpretation centres, an increase in associated jobs including rangers, council staff, labourers, garbage collectors, builders and plumbers is required to maintain the tracks and park facilities. Most of these positions are likely to come from the local community.

2 Distribution of Income to Local Communities

The purchase of goods and services not only increases employment opportunities, but also brings cash into the local community. Local goods and services include food, fuel, toiletries, camping supplies, alcohol, maps, books, tour guides, entertainment, and accommodation. The tourist dollar is a new dollar being injected into the local economy, bringing increased requirements for goods and services.

3 Greater Length of Stay of Ecotourists

Ecotourists tend to spend more time in one area than the traditional mass, packaged tourists who move on every day to a new place. They are also from higher socio-economic groups than most mass tourists. These two factors will tend to multiply the benefits listed above, increasing the income and employment opportunities to local communities.

4 Local Infrastructure and Accommodation Development

Visitor information and interpretation centres that cater for the needs of ecotourists are being developed in areas close to many popular national parks and reserves. Other infrastructure such as picnic and barbeque facilities, toilet blocks, tracks, access roads, hospitals, schools, and police stations will be built, improved, or have their capacity increased to cater for the needs of tourists and the growing residential community.

As ecotourists tend to stay longer in a region, extra accommodation may also be required. The construction and servicing of this infrastructure also provides local jobs and keeps more money in the community.

5 Generation of Income for Conservation

As mentioned earlier, many ecotourism operators utilise public land for most of their tours. In order to operate on this land they are required to meet certain criteria to obtain a permit from the land managers, including payment of a fee based on the number of clients they take in to the area, even where general public access is free. These fees are meant to contribute to the maintenance and development of the country's natural resources. The requirements differ from state to state, but the basic philosophy is the same.

Many ecotourism operators also contribute financially to conservation groups and activities such as reafforestation, noxious weed and pest control, and track maintenance in their region, as well as globally.

6 Additional Foreign Exchange Earnings

International inbound tourism is an export commodity. Many international visitors want to spend time in natural environments, and learn about the unusual Southern Hemisphere flora and fauna, bringing further income to country areas.

Rich Rewards of Tourism

Tasmania's tourism industry relies heavily on the state's natural environment and heritage, with ecotourism playing a major role. Estimates of the contribution of tourism to the Tasmanian economy in 1992 show the importance of tourism to the state.

The total contribution of tourism to employment was 17,290 people employed and $530,826,000.00 contributed to the aggregate income of the state. These figures include both direct and indirect contributions.

New Zealand is particularly rich in environmental wonders and diversity, ranging from glacial features to thermal activity. International tourism to New Zealand is growing at around twice the world rate of growth, with more than 1.5 million international visitors in 1996. The NZ Tourism Board has recognised that international tourists are becoming more interested in the environment, including ecotourism.

Tourism in New Zealand directly and indirectly employs more than 200,000 people.

Indirect Expenditure and Flow-on Effects

A major ethical aim of ecotourism is to spend money for goods and services locally. This makes it worth more to a community than other forms of tourism. The tourist dollar is a new dollar brought into the local community and some of it will be spent in that community. Obviously, the higher the proportion spent locally, the better off the community will be.

The first indirect flow-on effects to local communities are known as "production induced effects" which arise from businesses purchasing a range of goods and services from other firms in the region who in turn buy from others, and so on. The second are known as "consumption induced effects" where the staff employed acquire local goods and services for their own use as consumers, further stimulating the local economy.

The Tourism Multiplier

A range of "multipliers" has been developed that take these flow-on effects into account. Depending on the data assessed and the region involved, the multipliers in Australia and New Zealand range from a conservative 2.1 to 3.0. The National Centre for Studies on Travel and Tourism recommends a multiplier in the range of 2.5 to 3.0. This means that tourist expenditure of $100 per day would result in up to $300 flowing on to the local community.

9

> ## Tourism in the Daintree
>
> Aside from a handful of cattle, fruit and horticultural properties, most economic activity in the Daintree area of Far North Queensland arises from tourism. A study in the area in 1992 estimated that direct tourism expenditure was $17.9 million annually, with indirect flow-ons of $12.5 million, a total value of $30.4 million to the local economy each year.
>
> The tourism industry provided 290 permanent positions and 84 seasonal jobs, with most people employed by local tours and attractions run by small owner/operators. These operators, who worked part-time in the low season and full-time during the high season, had a small need for additional staff in peak times.
>
> The activities offered were all nature/ecotourism based, and included rainforest walks, night walks, environmental centres, river cruises on small vessels, horse riding, bike hire and four wheel drive tours.

Economic Yield of Tourism

The term "economic yield" has been used to express points of view that can be conflicting (or at least confusing), not unlike the use of statistics at times. "Yield" may be used in relation to the dollars that a tourist spends in a 24 hour period, as opposed to their overall expenditure. Thus a high-yield tourist may not stay for a long time, but will spend more per day than other tourists, clearing the way for more high-yield tourists to come into the region. However, tourism activity is usually centred around peak times and seasons, such as weekends and school holidays. So even though the "way has been cleared" for more tourists to arrive during the week, often they do not.

Encouraging tourists to stay longer than a weekend (say for three nights instead of two) will increase the overall expenditure from that tourist, even though daily expenditure (yield) will be a little less due to the offer of special accommodation rates. So, length of stay must be included in any discussion of economic yield in the tourism industry.

From a tourism point of view then, the term "yield" should incorporate both the daily expenditure and the length of stay. The good news about eco-tourism is that many ecotourists spend more per day than other nature-based tourists and stay longer than mass tourists, increasing both aspects of "yield".

Opportunity Costs

Although the economic benefits of ecotourism (and tourism in general) can be significant, once a decision is made to run a tourism operation, other choices, such as timber production or mining, are foregone (unless of course, these are part of the tourism product). While these opportunity costs are a consequence of all decisions, people often do not consider them when calculating the economic benefits of a tourism enterprise. Little research has been done in this area, but the table below compares cash returns from industries reliant on remnant vegetation with ecotourism.

Net Cash Returns from WA Wheatbelt Remnant Vegetation (1992/93):

Use	$ per operator day worked	$ per hectare
Wildflower Production	Up to 250	125–230
Ecotourism	50 –90	5–1500
Timber Products (fence posts)	150–575	not available
Timber Products (firewood)	65	20
Brushwood	not available	10–100
Seed Collection	15–120	not available

Source: ACIL (1993) Biodiversity Conservation and Sustainable Use Objectives

Of course, some of these activities, such as seed collection, could be combined with ecotourism, or incorporated into an ecotour itself as an activity. However, others, such as timber products and brushwood harvesting, would be lost with the development of ecotourism. The massive range in the value of ecotourism (between $5 and $1,500 per hectare) is too general to provide a basis for economic comparison, but the example shows some of the other industries that may be affected by ecotourism and demonstrates the wide range of income that it can generate.

Benefits Flow On From Quicksilver

Quicksilver Connections is a privately-owned marine day-tour company based in Port Douglas in Far North Queensland. From its beginnings as a small, family-run company in the early 1980s, it has grown into a multi-million dollar company, and one of the largest ecotourism operations in the country.

As a large company in the small town of Port Douglas, Quicksilver's potential for providing economic benefits to the community is substantial. The company has a policy of buying locally wherever possible and employs about 150 staff, from catering and boat crew through to reservations staff and marine biologists. Staff uniforms and Quicksilver souvenirs are designed and printed locally, weekly food purchases average $28,000 and fuel costs about $15,600 per week.

On a national scale, the company's vessels and pontoons are all Australian made, with many of them incorporating innovative Australian design such as the Wavepiercer catamaran, which was a Tasmanian concept, and the company's semi-submersibles that were designed and built in Cairns.

Environmental Benefits

As ecotourism places an economic value on the environment, the need for conservation and other environmental initiatives becomes not only possible but practical. This economic rationale can be used to expand protected natural areas and provides an incentive for private landowners to either maintain or return land to its natural state and to protect wildlife habitats.

Ecotourism also provides an environmentally sound alternative to unsustainable industries or industries that are no longer seen as appropriate for the area (such as high-polluting industries) and other damaging forms of tourism, such as mass tourism with its associated large-scale development and needs that are foreign to the region. For example, a golf course requires extensive use of herbicides and pesticides and large quantities of water to maintain its greens. In a dry area this would divert much-needed water away from farms, and pesticides and herbicides could potentially pollute the natural watercourses. An ecotourism style "resort" on the other hand, would not cater to this need, but would utilise the natural benefits of the region.

Tourism and Conservation: a Successful Combination

Earth Sanctuaries is a public company which demonstrates the success of partnerships between tourism and conservation. The company buys land, surrounds it with feral-proof fencing, eradicates the feral animals within the property (with particular attention to foxes and cats) and reintroduces indigenous wildlife. Earth Sanctuaries manages 80,000 hectares on six sites.

The company has raised development funds through the issue of shares, and meets the running costs of the sanctuaries through ecotourism — entrance fees to the sanctuaries, environmentally-friendly accommodation, and, most importantly, guided tours and environmental education.

Although shareholders have received only small dividends each year (due to the company's continued acquisition of land and conservation costs), the value of the shares has increased in ten years from $1 to $48 — a strong indication of the economic as well as ecological importance of ecotourism.

Intangible Benefits

In the current political climate of economic rationalism, benefits that cannot be directly quantified in monetary terms are often ignored. However, these intangible benefits are equally, and at times even more, important than "the bottom line". Ecotourism provides many intangible benefits that improve quality of life and often result in indirect economic and environmental benefits.

Local communities see that what they took for granted has a value and worth to other people — the view you wake up to every morning and the abundance of wildlife in your local forest take on a new meaning. The pride communities gain from "showing off" these things can change their whole feeling and attitude. You have probably visited a town where the residents tell you about special places to go and the things you can see in the immediate area — their civic pride shines.

Many rural areas are depressed because of a lack of employment opportunities. This depression is not just economic, but also exists in the low self-esteem of the under-employed people. Increased employment will improve individual self-esteem as well as community pride.

Our desire to move on from the past, and embrace modern appliances, computers and other machines, results in previous cultures being neglected and, at times, lost altogether. The role of ecotourism in cultural heritage encourages continued understanding of our older cultures, both indigenous and non-indigenous, maintaining important links with our heritage.

Many people in country areas are isolated from other cultures and other points of view. Increased tourism introduces them to people from other cultures and ways of life. The interaction is two-way — the visitors do not only learn about the area and people they are visiting, they also give their hosts information about their own cultures and beliefs. This is especially so for ecotourists, who are usually particularly interested in the local culture and environment.

Conclusion

Ecotourism can be defined as tourism that occurs in a natural setting, is educative and is managed in a sustainable manner. It is one of the fastest growing niche areas of tourism, and the broader tourism industry must adopt many of its values in order to survive in the long term.

Tourism, particularly ecotourism, provides many benefits to local communities. Ecotourism is a labour-intensive industry which can provide an alternative source of income, offer opportunities for young people in rural areas and create employment. It also provides opportunities for diversification, can reduce reliance on other industries, and lead to enhanced community facilities and infrastructure. Increasing the conservation ethic, highlighting the value of the natural environment, providing the local community with the opportunity to meet people from different areas and exchange ideas, increasing civic pride, and creating new business opportunities are also potential spin-offs from tourism in general and ecotourism in particular.

2 What is an Ecotourist?

It is important to understand the people who are interested in ecotourism, as it helps judge the likely appeal of a specific environmental attraction as well as developing a product that the ecotourist wants. There is no point in developing a business that takes people through a remote cave system in an adventurous, "caving" style if they are all elderly or cannot afford the cost of getting there. Marketing the product is also more effective when you understand who your market is, as will be discussed in Chapter 6.

People interested in the environment and in taking nature-based, ecological holidays come from a broad background, making it difficult to come up with a "typical ecotourist". However, studies have shown some similarities in those looking for ecotourism experiences.

Profile of an Ecotourist

First, both rural and urban dwellers have an interest in ecotourism, so do not assume that all your guests will be from major cities. People tend to forget sometimes that those living in country areas need to take a break as much as city people do. Obviously, their interest in the environment will be coloured by where they come from and how they earn a living — a Mallee farmer may be more interested in soil type and yield than a Sydney accountant (who, however, could still be interested in the yield aspect!).

Roy Morgan Value Segments

The most widely used segmentation of consumers in Australia are the Roy Morgan Value Segments, which are often used to identify various tourism markets. Several states and some New Zealand studies have used them. Like other market segmentations, the boundaries are somewhat arbitrary and will not fit in with everything. The two segments that appear to relate best to ecotourism are in the 35–49 age group, however, other research specifically on ecotourism suggests that the 40–54 age group are not active ecotourists.

Respondents to the survey are put into one of ten "value segments" based on their answers to a range of questions relating to their personal views and demographic reports (such as age, occupation, where they live, household income etc.). The two key value segments that have been identified as relating to ecotourism are the "Socially Aware" and "Visible Achievers".

The Socially Aware segment is aged between 35 and 49, the most educated of all the groups, employed as upmarket professionals earning over $45,000. They take a thoughtful and strategic approach to life. They are politically and socially active and environmentally aware.

The Visible Achievers are also aged between 35 and 49, working in upmarket professional positions and earning over $45,000. This group seeks recognition, status and evidence of success (such as cars, houses, expensive and unusual holidays).

Another segment that may also respond well to ecotourism, particularly the adventure-based products, is the "Young Optimists" who are the active, trendy, outgoing student generation aged between 18 and 24. They are trend setters, ambitious and career oriented, always collecting new experiences, ideas and relationships. They are often the children of the Visible Achievers or Socially Aware segments.

Knowledge of theses value segments may help you in developing and marketing your tourism product, but conduct some of your own research to see if these groups really do come to your region and are interested in your type of product. Research does not have to be complicated (leave that up to the Tourism Associations and marketing companies). By observing what people are doing and listening to them (tourists are usually extremely willing to talk about their experiences and ideas) you can get a great deal of information. Chapter 6 delves further into research and market segmentation.

Age

Ecotourists are usually in the 20–40 year age group, with a second large group, 55 years and older, indicating that the "mid-lifers" are looking for other forms of holiday. Many of the 40–54 year age group are still raising children, developing their careers and paying off mortgages. They have lower disposable income than the other groups, which may account for the lesser interest in ecotourism. This group will also be looking for family-oriented holidays that provide activities for their children as well as themselves.

Different types of ecotourism experiences tend to attract different types of individuals, particularly from the international market, which we will consider in more detail when we look at overseas tourists later in the chapter. Generally speaking, the younger age group of ecotourists (20–34 years old) tend to be more interested in adventurous ecotours, such as those involving white-water rafting or abseiling. There is little gender difference except that men show a slight bias towards cycling and women towards hiking. Equal numbers of men and women show interest in rafting. This gender balance is more even with ecotourists than for general tourists, suggesting that environmental appeal is non-sexist!

Education and Income

Generally speaking, ecotourists tend to be more educated than other tourists, showing an interest in learning about the environment, and earning higher incomes — usually associated with higher education levels. It is interesting to compare some figures here between the education levels of ecotourists and other tourists. In Australia, 20 per cent of ecotourists have a tertiary qualification whereas 12 per cent of other tourists are tertiary qualified, and 43 per cent of American ecotourists are graduates compared with 29 per cent of other tourists.

Some studies indicate that an even higher proportion of ecotourists are tertiary educated. One US study, for example, reported that a massive 82 per cent of "experienced" ecotourists were college graduates. However, there is evidence that the trend is shifting towards those with less education. It is important that we do not ignore this emerging group as they could well be the main ecotourists of the future.

Today's ecotourists have higher incomes than other tourists, and it has been suggested that they are also willing to pay more for their experience. This can be true, particularly when the tour offered is in a remote area with an interesting and fragile environment. But this does not mean that a tour operator can charge exorbitant rates and call anything an "ecotour". Some operators have tried to do this, but due to the educated nature of the ecotourist they are usually caught out when potential customers ask simple environmental questions, for example about their waste handling and minimal impact procedures.

Brochures produced by ecotourism associations and the government encourage tourists to ask such questions in order to ascertain the operator's commitment to the environment. The Ecotourism Association of Australia provides a brochure that is available to the general public, where ecotourists are encouraged to ask ecotour operators the following:

- Does the ecotourism operator comply with the EAA Code of Practice for Ecotourism Operators?

- Is a percentage of the economic benefit going back to or staying in the local community/environment?
- Does the tour operator use local guides, services and suppliers where possible?

Ecotourism operations in Australia have also adopted a range of industry standards which have been developed into an Ecotourism Accreditation program. Only approved operators can promote themselves as an "accredited ecotourism business/product". Chapter 6 provides details about this extremely important (and ground-breaking) area.

Environmental Behaviour of Ecotourists

Ecotourists are more likely to be involved in pro-environmental behaviour at home, such as recycling household waste and purchasing "green" products. Many of them belong to conservation organisations, but are not necessarily active in them, having a more "intellectual" interest in the environment, rather than hands-on experience. Research conducted by the Bureau of Tourism Research (BTR) showed that many ecotourists (about half of the people they interviewed) do not have very strong environmental concerns — they appreciate the environment and are interested in learning more, but are not necessarily committed to environmental protection.

This picture is quite different from the early ecotourist of the 1980s, who possessed a much stronger environmental ethic. Many of them worked on volunteer programs with scientists, naturalists and other groups, collecting data (such as the number and range of a particular plant species or activities of wildlife) and in projects such as reafforestation and land reclamation. These groups and tours still operate, particularly in South America, but the interest in ecotourism has broadened to encompass those who do not necessarily want such an intense "holiday", but still wish to support and learn about the environment.

Accommodation Preferences

Research conducted by Geelong Otway Tourism in Victoria found that ecotourists were more interested in staying in specialist accommodation in a natural setting such as farmstays, bed and breakfasts and private cottages than traditional motel style accommodation, which was regarded as highly undesirable. Studies in North America (a good source of international ecotourists) confirm this preference. Most ecotourists (60 per cent) prefer to stay in a cabin or lodge, closely followed by camping and bed and breakfasts.

When comparing some of the activities offered by specialist accommodation and traditional accommodation (such as motels and traditional resorts) at Port Douglas, the reasons why ecotourists prefer specialist accommodation are obvious:

Activities	Traditional accommodation (%)	Specialist accommodation (%)
Swimming	91.3	43.8
Tennis	21.7	25.0
Cycling	17.4	.2
Playground	4.3	6.2
Golf Course	8.6	0
Gymnasium	4.3	0
Rainforest Walks	0	50.0
Wildlife Viewing	0	25.0
Guided Walks	0	25.0
Horse Riding	0	18.8
Snorkelling	0	12.5
Marked Trails	0	12.5
Library	12.5	0
Beach Walks	0	6.2
Nature Photos	0	6.2
Average number of activities offered at each place:	1.7	3.1

Source: Moscardo, G., Morrison, A.M., and Pearce, P.L. (1996), *Specialist Accommodation and Ecologically-Sustainable Tourism*, in **Journal of Sustainable Tourism, 4** (3), 1996.

These two distinct types of accommodation appear to be targeting two very different types of tourists, with the specialist accommodation offering more of the activities and interests that motivate ecotourists, such as wildlife viewing and guided walks. The specialist accommodation tends to be more interactive, whereas traditional accommodation provides more static facilities and infrastructure such as golf courses, libraries and gymnasiums.

Seasonality

Where "general tourists" favour definite seasons at most destinations, ecotourists tend to travel all year round and are not as seasonally biased. There could be many reasons for this trend, but most active ecotourists are in the age groups where they probably have not had families yet or their children have grown up (the "empty-nesters"), suggesting they are more flexible and less reliant on school holidays. Also, their interest in the environment makes ecotourists less susceptible to what others may consider bad weather — the tropical wet season can be of more interest to ecotourists than perfect sunshine every day.

Potential vs Actual Ecotourists

Australians' and New Zealanders' interest in ecotourism seems to be greater than their actual rate of participation, indicating that gains can be made by increasing the awareness of domestic tourists about the range, quality and quantity of ecotourism experiences available in Australia and New Zealand. The Bureau of Tourism Research found that Queenslanders were the most likely group to visit a natural area (64 per cent of the population), closely followed by Western Australians, New South Welshmen, South Australians, Victorians and Tasmanians (38 per cent). Of course, they are not necessarily going to visit these areas in their own state, but will travel to other states as well.

These "potential ecotourists" are interested in taking a holiday that is nature-based and follows the principles of ecotourism, but have never actually done so. Research conducted by BTR indicates that potential ecotourists actually have a broader profile than those already participating in ecotourism. For example, while actual ecotourists are more likely to have college qualifications and earn over $40,000, potential ecotourists do not differ from the general population.

The reasons why these potential ecotourists have not participated in ecotours are numerous. For example, the range and type of tours offered may not be broad enough, particularly for older people who tend to prefer four wheel drive tours to hiking tours (with some exceptions!). More importantly, they may not even be aware that the tours or products exist, the information not being made readily available to the broader tourism market. Also, people in the mid-life group who are interested in ecotours may be restricted by family and financial considerations if they have dependent children.

In order to capture this broader market and increase the appeal and awareness of ecotourism, it is important to look at the region(s) you are operating in and find out who is coming, why, and the reasons that others are going somewhere else. Much of this information is readily available from regional and state tourist associations. The role of tourist associations is covered in Chapter 6 under the heading "Networking".

This case study shows that just about every group of people that visits a national park contains elements of ecotourism, and shows that the potential ecotourism market is big. It also highlights some marketing issues — your total product will not appeal to everyone, even though some elements of it may, so you will need to decide which part of the ecotourism market you are targeting. Even if you do not totally embrace ecotourism, your product will have a stronger appeal if it incorporates at least some of the elements.

Identifying Potential Ecotourists

As the gateway to the Grampians National Park in Western Victoria, Halls Gap is a well-known, nature-based, ecotourism destination where the number of visitors has grown considerably in the past few years. Concerns have been expressed that the pressure of increased visitation may result in both environmental and social changes that may decrease, or even destroy, the attraction of the place.

As ecotourism is a form of tourism that aims to safeguard the environment and benefit the local community, while also providing a rich experience for visitors, the managers of the Park felt that it would be a desirable form of tourism to encourage. However, because little is known about the nature of ecotourists, research was undertaken to identify this "preferred" type of tourist (ecotourist) so that they could be encouraged while discouraging those less preferred.

A group of Masters of Environmental Science students from Monash University and a consultant were contracted to undertake the study. They identified the following seven distinct groups visiting Halls Gap and the Grampians:

1 **Young, carefree, have a good time**

Nature is the background for their activity, seen as a physical resource for the exploits of youth. This group has a major impact on the park, requiring infrastructure and services, particularly in the adventure and entertainment areas.

2 **Keen, active consumers of National Park and facilities**

Keen learners and want to do the right thing. Generally family groups who utilise interpretation and learning activities as well as adventure and entertainment. They appreciate accommodation that provides open fires, spas, restaurants or gourmet camping. This group is the largest at Halls Gap.

3 **Self contained/self regulated**

The National Park is a great resource and place to get away from the stress of everyday life. Not keen on the controls placed on them in the National Park, and consider their behaviour as responsible and not requiring control. Highly educated group with a penchant for four wheel drives and self-reliance. This is another large group.

4 **Budget group traveller**

One quarter of this group are from overseas. They have shorter but more active stays and are prepared to do things with fewer "frills" — the security and camaraderie of the group seems to compensate. They are interested in visiting the major icons of the park.

5 **My Bush, my 4WD**

The National Park is a great resource and a place to get away from the everyday. They are not keen on the controls in the park, and are more interested in socialising and relaxing by their car than bushwalking. They are a bit "larrikinish" and not interested in interpretation of the environment.

6 **Informed independent traveller**

One-fifth of this group were international travellers and it contained fewer Victorians than other groups. They show the most interest in learning more about the environment and indigenous culture. They appreciate the unique features of the place and are concerned that careful management is employed to protect them.

7 **Thrifty unadventurous family tourer**

Seem to be separate from nature, appreciating its beauty but not interested in experiencing it.

The research team felt that Groups 2, 4 and 6 had the most ecotourism potential, with Group 2 having a keen interest in learning, Group 4 also for their interest in learning and their willingness to modify their behaviour and Group 6 with their keenness to learn about nature and culture and interest in responsible management of the land. However, there was no single, easily identifiable "ecotourist", with elements of ecotourism being found in many of the groups, and potential in others.

Another relevant finding was the general reluctance to pay for interpretive sessions, even though there was a strong desire to learn about nature and culture. People seemed to prefer to purchase a publication than experience a live story, reflecting a desire for self-discovery and independence.

Conclusion

The research team concluded that it was not possible to simply encourage one group of visitor and discourage another in order to sustain the environment as all the groups had some "ecotourist" potential.

Source: Plumeridge et al, Ecotourism Association of Australia Conference Papers, 1996

The International Ecotourist

Different nationalities and cultures have different attitudes towards travel and the environment. Apart from cultural differences, their stage in the "tourist life-cycle" often reflects the type of tourism they are interested in. Generally speaking, groups that are new to travelling tend to move around en masse on extremely structured tours. They are interested in seeing the main tourist icons and keeping a photographic record of every stage of their holiday. In New Zealand as well as in Australia, this typifies many Asian tourists, most notably the Japanese. However, as they move on from being "first time" travellers, they become more adventurous, seeking alternative experiences and deeper cultural interaction. Many more Japanese tourists are now travelling independently and off the beaten track, while other Asian groups, newer to travelling, are choosing mass tours.

A deciding factor for choosing an ecotour is the length of stay in the country. With only a few days, a tourist will tend to avoid nature-based tours that are of a longer duration, such as many (but not all) ecotours. The average length of stay in Australia of the following nationalities who visited national parks (indicating some interest in the environment) is extremely important:

Switzerland & Scandinavia	56 nights
United Kingdom and Ireland	47 nights
Canada	44 nights
Germany	41 nights
United States	28 nights
Japanese	9 nights

The Japanese have a very limited time available (dictated by their short annual leave), whereas the Swiss average just under two months in Australia (with more students and retirees travelling). Looking at this list in light of what these groups are doing while in Australia starts to give a picture of the international ecotourism market.

In the age groups of 20–40 years and 55+ years (classic ecotourism age group) three-quarters of all Swiss tourists visit a national park, with at least two-thirds of Germans, Canadians, and Scandinavians also visiting the parks. The largest group to undertake outback safaris are from UK and Ireland, who also have the greatest number of bush walkers and rock climbers (the United States being a close second).

European visitors tend to travel widely in Australia and New Zealand in both urban and rural areas, whereas the Japanese tend to concentrate their nature-based experiences around major attractions such as Rotorua, Uluru, or the Phillip Island penguin parade, which is also close to a major city. While the Japanese are not considered to be overly adventurous, they are more likely to go snorkelling or scuba diving than bushwalking, and make up over one-third of the dive market.

The nationalities with the lowest propensity to visit national parks are the Japanese, other Asians and New Zealanders visiting Australia. This does not mean that the Japanese do not visit national parks, far from it — they are the highest number of people visiting national parks, but the lowest percentage, and they mainly visit those parks close to cities or the major tourist icons. The low proportion of New Zealanders may also be a surprise, considering the emphasis on the environment in that country, but many New Zealand visitors come for the city-based cultural activities such as shopping and theatre and to visit friends and relatives. However, this market should not be neglected as they are close to Australia and tend to visit regularly. A higher percentage of Australians in New Zealand tend to undertake outdoor/nature-based activities. Australia is New Zealand's main source of international visitors, followed by the USA, UK and Japan respectively.

COUNTRY OF RESIDENCE

Attraction	United States	Canada	UK & Ireland	Other Europe	Japan	Other Asia	New Zealand	Other
NEW SOUTH WALES								
National Parks	75,700	12,600	72,300	72,300	139,300	98,600	36,300	27,000
Beaches outside Sydney	28,600	7,900	49,200	45,000	13,900	26,000	30,400	12,000
Farm experiences	8,200	3,400	4,800	6,500	14,100	16,500	2,300	1,500
Aboriginal culture/ attractions	6,800	1,900	8,100	9,000	2,300	4,000	800	1,400
VICTORIA								
Phillip Island/ Penguin Parade	25,800	5,200	21,100	31,600	44,200	70,300	14,900	7,100
Twelve Apostles/ Great Ocean Road	17,100	3,700	23,400	34,400	7,800	24,800	6,600	3,800
Grampians National Park	4,400	1,500	7,500	11,200	900	6,700	3,600	1,100
QUEENSLAND								
Stradbroke/ Moreton Bay/Islands	5,600	1,200	5,300	5,000	200	1,000	4,500	1,000
Fraser Island/ Hervey Bay	10,400	3,900	19,000	40,200	1,600	1,500	6,500	3,000
Green/Fitzroy Islands	16,400	6,100	18,400	21,200	90,300	5,100	3,600	2,300
Whitsunday Islands	21,400	9,800	21,500	39,100	34,000	5,600	4,700	2,300
Daintree/ Cape Tribulation	30,300	7,400	26,200	39,900	4,300	2,000	6,100	2,600
Queensland National Parks	37,500	8,000	43,100	53,700	23,800	13,900	30,200	8,300
Outback/Stockman's Hall of Fame	3,900	1,300	2,800	8,400	300	0	200	400
SOUTH AUSTRALIA								
Cleland Wildlife Park	3,900	1,500	11,400	7,700	2,800	4,600	2,900	900
Flinders/Wilpena Pound/Arkaroola	800	900	4,900	10,500	0	600	1,500	900
Kangaroo Island	4,300	1,800	5,000	14,400	1,800	2,200	1,200	200

Attraction	United States	Canada	UK & Ireland	Other Europe	Japan	Other Asia	New Zealand	Other
WESTERN AUSTRALIA								
Rottnest Island	4,500	2,100	19,900	10,900	6,600	9,800	3,000	2,300
Yanchep/Sun City/ Yanchep Nat. Park	1,400	700	15,500	7,100	2,400	20,100	3,400	1,400
Monkey Mia/Shark Bay	1,400	700	6,500	13,600	1,300	2,700	1,800	300
The Pinnacles	2,600	800	10,500	16,700	14,400	14,000	4,300	700
Wave Rock	2,100	800	6,300	9,300	1,200	7,900	1,700	600
Margaret River/ Wineries	1,600	2,000	14,700	11,100	1,000	12,100	3,500	2,200
Pemberton/ Karri Forests	2,600	900	8,600	9,100	900	7,500	1,400	1,400
TASMANIA								
Maria Island	600	400	200	900	0	200	0	100
Gordon River	900	700	7,500	2,600	1,100	700	3,100	200
Cradle Mountain Nat. Park	4,000	900	9,900	4,700	1,200	3,600	2,200	500
NORTHERN TERRITORY								
Litchfield Park	4,500	2,500	5,700	22,100	1,200	2,100	900	1,000
Kakadu National Park	11,500	4,600	13,000	48,700	3,600	2,400	800	1,400
Nitmuluk (Katherine Gorge)	5,100	4,400	9,800	33,800	1,200	2,100	1,200	900
Devils Marbles	1,900	2,600	5,400	17,200	700	400	500	900
Simpson Gap/Stanley Chasm/Glen Helen	6,200	3,400	11,000	17,400	400	500	800	1,500
Uluru (Ayers Rock)	28,700	9,400	35,700	72,000	32,900	3,500	1,100	3,200
Kings Canyon	6,500	3,900	14,000	34,700	2,500	1,300	1,000	1,000
AUSTRALIAN CAPITAL TERRITORY								
Tidbinbilla	4,700	1,300	2,900	3,000	200	3,300	0	800

Source: BTR International Visitor Survey, 1993

The Bureau of Tourism Research conducts an International Visitor Survey (IVS) that interviews 15,000 international tourists annually as they are leaving the country. The survey is extensive and provides a great deal of important information on international tourists — where they have been, how much they spent, how long they stayed etc. To obtain ecotourism data, the BTR has modified this information and produced a table that lists visitor numbers to selected state attractions by international tourists. These state attractions were chosen as the ones most likely to offer nature-based/ecotourism experiences from the data available, and are by no means exclusive. If your area or region is not listed, it does not mean you do not have any ecotourism potential, but the information does give some indication of interest in some areas and types of ecotourism from particular nationalities.

The international tourism market can be an expensive and time-consuming one to enter and to service, so it is best to first get your product right by concentrating on the domestic market, then to consider whether the international market is for you. For most tourism operators, international tourists are the icing on the cake, with domestic tourists accounting for at least three-quarters of their business. However, it is worth considering where this market may be and what the different national groups are interested in during the planning stages of your tourism product. There is no point in planning for a future Asian market if they are not there in the first place. This important issue is discussed in more detail in Chapter 6.

The BTR has also noted a growth in participation in outback safaris by some international groups, with 47 per cent more Germans and 21 per cent more Swiss taking safaris over the past few years. The rest of Europe has also increased its participation by 44 per cent, indicating that there is significant growth in "hard" ecotourism activities in these international markets. This, of course is assuming that outback safaris operate by ecotourism principles and standards. Many already do, and more are coming to recognise the benefits of providing an "eco" experience.

Motivators

People travel for a number of reasons, or "motivators". It may be stress release, social stimulation or a desire for personal fulfilment. The recommendation of a friend is an extremely powerful motivator, with "word of mouth" being the single most important marketing device in tourism. Many people return to an area to experience something they missed on a previous visit.

Some differences exist between the motivators of ecotourists and general tourists. Ecotourists are likely to be attracted by: escape from the demands of life to a simpler lifestyle, rediscovering their "self", learning about nature and doing something adventurous and daring. Non-ecotourists, or general tourists, tend to be more interested in being together as a family (reflecting the age group differences), feeling at home away from home and doing nothing. The desire to experience things rather than just look at them from a distance is becoming increasingly important to all tourists, especially ecotourists.

Exploring the Differences

According to a study of Kangaroo Island in South Australia, there are differences between what motivates the international nature-based tourist and the national (from other states) and state (South Australian) ecotourist. The following table lists the activities that each group wishes to undertake in order of preference:

International Tourist	National Tourist	State Tourist
1 See natural wonders	Know and experience own country	Improve knowledge of state
2 Visit a farm	Experience wildlife in its natural state	Wining and dining
3 Attend an unusual event	Experience living history	Meeting other people
4 Shop for local arts and crafts	Shop for local produce, arts and crafts	Activities for children
5 See/interact with wildlife	Try new food and wine	Night time activities
6 Try new food	Experience beaches or Fishing the outdoors	
7 Meet some locals	Plenty to see and do	Bushwalking
8 Photo opportunities	Warm, pleasant weather	——

Source: Manidis Roberts Consultants, Developing a Tourism Optimisation Management Model, 1996

This survey shows some distinct differences between the desires and motivations of ecotourists, from international, national and state areas, indicating that the international tourists are less focussed on recreational activity and more interested in viewing and experiencing the unique natural wonders of the area.

It also raises the question of whether domestic tourists are less interested in the natural environment, or more blase than international tourists. It has often been noted that local visitors to an area express surprise at discovering and learning more about the environment they thought they knew. It is a challenge for tour operators to convey this message to domestic tourists.

Range of Activities for Ecotourists

As many ecotourists are looking for a range of activities, some of the elements that could be included in an ecotourism product are:

Wilderness setting
Wildlife viewing
Wildflower and other flora viewing
Hiking/trekking with qualified guides
Visiting a national park or other protected area (particularly if it is not accessible to the general public)
Rafting/canoeing/kayaking
Scuba diving/snorkelling

Casual walking
Photography
Interaction with other cultures
Physically challenging programs with qualified and experienced guides
Interpretive programs
Sailing
Cycling
Horse Riding
Cross-country skiing
Mountain and rock climbing/abseiling
Fishing

Such activities could be built around an environmental festival as well as standard tourism attractions or accommodation. Festivals and special events play a major role in local communities, providing them with increased revenue and many of the benefits outlined in the previous chapter. Special events are studied in more detail in Chapter 3.

Information and Education Needs of Ecotourists

Many tourists do not plan or expect to learn anything on their holiday and they may be surprised at what they do learn accidentally or incidentally. However, with ecotourism, some learning or education is anticipated. It may be structured or otherwise according to the needs of the tourists and the type of tour.

The term "interpretation" is often used when tourist education is discussed. It is preferable to "education" as it implies that some sense is made of what is being experienced. For example, rather than just pointing out the features of a plant, the nature of the plant is "interpreted" by explaining how it fits into the ecosystem and its relationship with other plants and animals.

Environmental interpretation in the context of ecotourism has two aspects: learning about the ecology of an area and learning about the sensitive nature of the environment with ways to minimise impacts of tourism. Education on minimising the impacts of tourism will probably be demonstrated by the operators, who will need to manage impacts themselves, whether they are running a tour, accommodation, attraction, or even a special event.

Learning about nature and the ecology of an area can take many forms, from "gazing" at nature through to interacting with the environment. Gazing at a wombat or alpine flower will provide the "gazer" with a learning experience, by observing how the wombat reacts to human actions and seeing aspects of the flower, such as whether it faces the sun or is shaded. The information gained by gazing may be sufficient for many tourists and can provide as much learning as some interactive educational programs, especially if it is combined with timely information from the tour guide or operator.

When learning, people remember 20 per cent of what they hear, 30 per cent of what they see, 50 per cent of what they hear and see, and 70 per cent of what they do. So a combination of interpretive techniques will provide your clients with the most effective and interesting learning experience.

Verbal Interpretation

Most verbal interpretation is provided at the actual site, where short presentations can describe particular features as they occur and bring them into context rather than talking about them later in a purely theoretical way. Questions are answered as they arise, and much relevant information can be provided in a format that is interesting and easy to retain by using the combination of seeing, hearing and doing.

Verbal information can also be provided through lectures that may be given prior to the tour, at information nights, on the way to the site during the tour, or after the tour. Slides are an effective tool to use with lectures and provide a visual reference, increasing the retention rate and interest level of the audience. Larger operators who need to inform big groups, or operators with special interest or study groups (eg a team of naturalists, historians or ecology students) tend to use lectures the most.

Presenting a Lecture

Most adults have an attention span of between 25 and 40 minutes, and can only process between five and nine pieces of information at a time (known as the "seven plus or minus two rule"). They forget most of what is said within a few hours. Practical reinforcement is effective, but it needs to be provided within those first few hours. So, a 30 minute presentation that has too many items of information will seem too long, even though it is within the attention span limits. It is preferable to keep the lecture short with the opportunity for questions and further information to be provided afterwards. Remember, your guests are on holiday and may not want to be over-burdened with "dry" learning such as interminable lectures.

There are four basic learning styles, with most people falling into one or two categories. These have been described as the tortoise, the philosopher, the hare and the entrepreneur. You should consider each of the styles and incorporate aspects of all of them in your presentation.

The tortoise prefers theory and tends to be slow in speech (but not wit) and responds well to structured information. The philosopher is also a slow speaker and looks for practical evidence. Both of these types are unlikely to speak out or ask questions, but they want detailed information that could be provided through a small, relevant reference collection.

The hare prefers to learn from hands-on experience and speaks fast and forcefully, whilst the entrepreneur is interested in the "big picture" and has an enthusiastic and warm personality. Both these types are looking for an overall view, with the entrepreneur particularly wanting to learn something unusual.

Interpreting the Reef

Quicksilver Connections, a large marine day-tour operator in Far North Queensland provides tours to the Great Barrier Reef for a wide range of tourists and prides itself on its standard of interpretive services. The company uses a combination of interpretive techniques, which enables it to provide information at all levels of interest.

The company employs marine biologists who provide interpretation and education. On the way out to the reef, all visitors are briefed on appropriate behaviour (such as not standing on coral or souveniring pieces). This talk is combined with lectures on the ecology of the reef. At the reef the biologists actively guide snorkelling tours and beach walks and maintain a vigilant eye on their guests, correcting their behaviour if necessary.

On the return journey the biologists are available to answer any questions arising from the reef visit, and an on-board library is available to answer more detailed queries.

As well as employing specialists, all the tourism staff at Quicksilver are trained in basic reef-based biology through an in-house education program. This increases the number of people able to educate and interpret at the broader level desired by many of the guests, and provides a continuity of information from the desk staff through to the on-board hosts and crew.

Static Interpretation

Static interpretation may take the form of self-guided walks with information signs, explanatory brochures and displays. Tours may be personalised by guides using this information, and providing more in-depth information.

Councils and government conservation departments provide many of the on-site static displays and signs in public areas such as national parks and council reserves. If you are taking people to such areas and would like to see a higher level of information provided, it may be worthwhile making a submission to the appropriate body (council or national parks body, for example).

If you are operating on your own property, consider introducing some displays and signs that will provide your guests with introductory information. This will reduce the number of questions directed at you and at the same time raise the awareness of all your guests, not just those who ask. Many local and state governments are providing excellent signage and displays, so looking at how they present the material should provide you with plenty of inspiration.

The signs used at some vantage points with a panoramic view are good examples of effective signage. A diagram of the vista is provided, with important landmarks marked on the sign so that tourists know what they are seeing.

Interpretation centres and displays are usually the domain of larger tourist attractions, but there is no reason why smaller versions cannot be presented that focus on a specific theme on your own property. Once again, by visiting other tourist attractions, particularly some ecotourist or nature-based attractions, such as sanctuaries and zoos (many of which have excellent signage) you will get ideas for your own display. Many tourism operators incorporate a display into a guest meeting area, where they may include photos of past tours or "experiences". (These photos are also great public relations, as past guests usually love to see photos of themselves in such a display!)

As well as signage and displays, brochures and fliers providing interpretive material can be developed and printed at minimal cost. Information can range from written historical and environmental detail through to glossy photos of local flora and fauna.

Pre and Post Experience Information

Different people require their information at different stages of a holiday. Some prefer to research as much as they can beforehand whereas others become more interested in a particular place after they have been there. Another group will want all the information served up to them whilst they are there. So information and interpretation must be available at all stages of the tour.

State environment departments and national parks services have already produced a great deal of information which is readily available and can be used as pre and post experience material. Some operators provide a suggested reading list of publications relevant to their tourism product when bookings are confirmed, enabling the tortoise and philosopher types to undertake the prior research they so enjoy.

During the tour (or stay), a small library can provide many answers to those often-asked questions, and publications identifying birds, wildlife and flora are invaluable. Another excellent form of information can be provided through personal knowledge and efforts, such as photographing the flowers at a particular site and providing brief notes about them. Anecdotes and historical information can also be included, personalising the information beyond text books.

A follow-up letter with some additional information on features of their holiday will not only be of interest to most of your customers but will provide you with bonus points on your customer service. The impact of public relations of this kind cannot be over-stated, and will be re-examined in Chapter 6.

How Important is Interpretation to the Ecotourist?

Only a limited amount of research is available to assess how ecotourists feel about interpretation and learning about nature. What has been done shows that although ecotourists are highly motivated by learning, it is still less important than looking, resting, smelling, listening, experiencing and exploring. So, simple nature appreciation and gazing appears to be more important than detailed learning, but much can be learnt through the use of these subtle, hands-on techniques. In support of this view, tourists surveyed in New South Wales rated "giving the mind a rest" slightly ahead of "learning about nature". Keep this in mind and don't overload your guests with too much information — be selective and relevant.

Ecotourists are the group most likely to display an active interest in learning about nature, and those who are most interested tend to be the most knowledgeable, so further information should be available for them. However, as the market becomes broader, the number of less knowledgeable ecotourists is likely to increase. The educational needs of this group are probably closer to the research findings above, with gazing and appreciation being important. You may need to provide information at a range of levels and detail to the same group —- continually holding a group up to respond to detailed technical questions from one member will soon result in everyone else becoming bored and losing interest.

Direct Involvement

Nature-based tourists have also shown a desire to become involved in day-to-day tour activities such as carrying and setting up equipment, preparing meals and removing obstacles (such as logs across tracks). This can also be a learning activity for many people who have not undertaken these tasks before, and is an excellent opportunity to provide education on minimal impact techniques.

When providing opportunities for guests to participate in the direct operating of the tour or experience, be careful not to make everyone feel obliged to help (unless this is clearly stated in your promotional material). Also, keep in mind your legal responsibilities towards your guests, in particular safety and hygiene. If the work is at all dangerous, supervise them carefully and if they are dealing with food make sure they understand hygiene procedures. If they are helping with equipment (particularly in relation to adventure activities), check the equipment personally before permitting its use. Your guests' safety and well-being is your responsibility, no-one else's.

Feedback

To find out if you are meeting your guests' interpretation requirements, question them either directly or with an exit survey. Find out what they were interested in learning as well as what they actually learnt. If you are contacting them directly, do so about one week after the end of the tour, so they have time to assimilate their experience. Of course, many people when contacted directly will be disinclined to give any negative feedback, so often an anonymous questionnaire is a better way of getting more honest feedback.

An exit survey should not be extensive — just one page of questions with a "tick the box" or other simple format. This makes it easy for your clients to complete and also for you to evaluate. By providing room for comments, more qualitative information can be obtained. Below is a sample survey form for a tour — this is an example only and if you decide to follow it, the questions should be modified to suit your particular needs.

Conclusion

Although it is not easy to draw up a single profile of today's ecotourist, he/she tends to be aged between 20 and 40 or over 55, well educated, and possessing a basic conservation ethic. The most important thing that ecotourists want from a holiday is to experience nature close-up, with a small group of like-minded people. They are generally attracted to an area for its intrinsic natural worth, with the environment dominating the ecotourist rather than tourism dominating the environment. Issues such as avoiding environmental damage and supporting the local economy are increasing in importance as ecotourists become more experienced and learn from other travellers and operators.

The wish to enjoy scenery and nature increases rapidly the more experienced the traveller becomes, with first-time travellers tending to go to man-made and cultural attractions. The mainstream tourism market appears to be following the ecotourists' lead. For example, the dolphins at Monkey Mia in Western Australia are now on all major touring itineraries in the region, whereas they were initially a nature-based, ecotourism attraction.

Although people on ecotours wish to be close to nature, appreciating and observing it and getting away from the masses, they do not necessarily want to learn about detailed scientific phenomena — it is important to tailor the educational component to the group. Education on correct behaviour in the bush and appropriate waste management techniques may be enough learning. Remember, they are on holiday and may wish to rest their brains!

SAMPLE CLIENT SURVEY FORM

TOUR .... DEPARTURE DATE ....

| Range of activities offered | [ ] Not enough | [ ] As expected | [ ] Too much |

Comments ....

| Staff courtesy | [ ] Excellent | [ ] OK | [ ] Poor |

Comments ....

| Staff knowledge of nature | [ ] Excellent | [ ] Adequate | [ ] Not enough |

Comments ....

| Staff knowledge of minimal impact practices | [ ] Excellent | [ ] Adequate | [ ] Poor |

Comments ....

| How well did the staff pass on information? | [ ] Very Well | [ ] OK | [ ] Not at all |

Comments ....

| Pacing of the learning activities | [ ] Too easy | [ ] Fine | [ ] Too difficult |

Comments ....

| Suitability of facilities | [ ] Excellent | [ ] Good | [ ] Poor |

Comments ....

| How would you rate the tour overall? | [ ] Excellent | [ ] Good | [ ] Poor |

Comments ....

How did you find out about the tour?

....

In order to assist us to understand our clients better, would you please complete the following.

Age Group: [ ] under 20 [ ] 20-25 [ ] 26-30 [ ] 31-35 [ ] 36-40 [ ] 41-50 [ ] 50+

Sex: [ ] male [ ] female   Have you travelled with us before? Yes/No

You came on the tour with: [ ] partner [ ] friend [ ] group of friends [ ] family [ ] singly

Thank you for your cooperation

3 Working with the Local Community

The growth in tourism over the past 15 or so years has increased pressure on some local communities, particularly in environmentally and culturally sensitive areas. These places tend to be the most popular with tourists as they offer different and rare experiences. One of the best known and documented of these is Uluru, where early tourism included an air strip and motel next to the rock, causing environmental, noise and visual pollution, and alienating the local Aboriginal community which was forced to bow to tourist pressure, with no say in the running of the attraction. This has changed since the Aborigines were granted ownership of the park and the motel and airstrip removed. It is an excellent example of the potential dangers of tourism and the possible ways of resolving them.

Complex relationships exist between all the tourism stakeholders — tourists, residents, investors, tour operators, non-government and government organisations. Often the local communities feel disenfranchised and forgotten in the rush for the tourist dollar. Hundreds of examples exist where the rapid growth of tourism in an area has caused the local residents to lose the very attributes that attracted them there in the first place. This does not have to be the case, however. With community consultation and sensitive planning, many of the negative aspects of tourism growth can be minimised. This is one of the main elements of ecotourism.

What is a "Community"?

"Communities" are often talked about, and most of us have a sense of what the word means, but what is it exactly? A community contains both physical and emotional elements, starting with the point it occupies in a particular area, which can be bounded physically by geographic landmarks such as rivers and mountains or simply by the proximity of the population, as in a small town. The community has a system of social organisation and activities and common ties ranging from family and heritage through to making a living in similar ways (from the land, the sea, logging, mining etc.). A community has a "sense of place", within the landscape and/or historically and usually possesses a range of traditions and values.

The above description can be applied to both indigenous and non-indigenous communities, large and small. Most of the elements of a community revolve around emotional rather than physical aspects, such as the sense of belonging, heritage, sense of place and social organisation. It is easy to overlook these more intangible areas when considering a tourism development (which includes guided tours and activities, not just resorts) as they are not easy to quantify. However, to have a sustainable tourism industry that is around for many years to come these aspects of community must be carefully considered.

The community may also include non-residents who have an emotional link with the area. These may people who have taken their annual holidays in the area for generations and activity-based groups such as horse riders, bush walkers, canoeists, or conservationists and naturalists. They are all stakeholders and should be considered as part of the overall tourism community if problems are to be avoided. Many of these groups are highly motivated to resist change that may affect their level of enjoyment or participation.

Working Together in the Rainforest

Mait's Rest, a beautiful rainforest gully in the Otway National Park, Victoria is an example of community cooperation, and cooperation between the land management agency, Natural Resources and Environment (NRE) and tour operators. The area is close to a highway, making it very popular and accessible, and leading to degradation and damage. NRE realised that the place would continue to be used due to its easy access, so set about repairing degraded areas and improving the walking track to minimise its impact on the rainforest. The park managers explained to the local community how they were planning to protect the forest, and gained community support for the project.

The severely graded track was re-aligned and a raised boardwalk and viewing platform constructed. Now, one of the local tour operators voluntarily keeps the gutter area of the boardwalk clear of leaf litter to enable proper channelling of water run-off, thus reducing the potential for erosion.

There are many examples where tour operators and local community groups are assisting the land management agencies in their work, with such cooperation improving relationships and understanding between the various groups.

Community Support/Participation

Residents (especially those in small communities) are often against tourism, fearing an influx tourists and their interests, and the possibility of being exploited by the larger tourism concerns. Locals also fear that the character of their community will change and that their quality of life will be eroded, with tourism not only altering the nature of the place, but also introducing petty crime and prostitution. The Gold Coast area of Queensland, for example, 20 years ago was a quiet holiday spot for Queenslanders, whereas today it is a conglomeration of high-rise holiday apartments, casinos and nightclubs, with an alarming level of petty crime, a huge number of unemployed people who moved to the area in search of work, and an almost invisible local community.

This should not be how ecotourism (or any tourism) is run today, and even on the Gold Coast values are shifting towards consideration of the environment. Couran Cove, a resort development at the north end of the Gold Coast is an example. The resort is a move away from the standard man-made swimming pools and canals towards land reclamation and reafforestation, with walks, nature-based activities, and efficient and effective waste and energy management. Chapter 5 contains an extensive case study of Couran Cove.

All tourism needs community support, but particularly nature-based and ecotourism as they are so often closely linked with the local community. An understanding of the needs of the local community is crucial, and if it is your own community, remember that it will include other people who may feel differently to you — they have as much right as you to be considered. Consultation and cooperation between local government, the business community, farmers and individuals is essential because of the nature of ecotourism. The attractions being promoted to the tourist are often those that are also highly prized by the community.

Taking Time to Consult

Consultation proved effective for a proposed resort at Tairua in New Zealand. The developers held discussions with the relevant authorities, Department of Conservation, tangata whenua (the major Maori decision-making tribe), the New Zealand Tourism Board, the regional tourism association, neighbours to the site, the local environmental group, community board and ratepayers association.

Public concerns were raised about traffic congestion, access, adequacy of drainage, disruption to peace and quiet, and intrusion by helicopters. The tangata whenua wanted native trees to be safeguarded, a sacred site on the area to be identified and a guarantee that development would stop if cultural sites were encountered.

The developers incorporated conditions that satisfied all the interest groups into the proposal and they were given permission to proceed.

Generating this support may not be easy and will probably take some time, but if the locals have the opportunity to voice their concerns and opinions and also to offer some solutions, they will be more likely to support an ecotourism venture. Involving the local community in aspects of the venture will also create a more positive atmosphere, and while consensus won't always be possible, acceptable solutions can be achieved through consultation.

Opportunities for local involvement can range from the planning and development stage through to the operation of the business. The community should be able to participate in each stage of the planning process. As well as actually working on the project, local members of the community could sit on advisory boards, tourism planning committees and participate directly in the management of the project (depending on the size of the venture). Community groups that may be interested in participating include chambers of commerce, conservation groups, ratepayer associations, historical societies, recreational clubs (bushwalking, climbing, sailing etc.), service clubs, progress associations and senior citizen groups.

Barossa Community Tuned into Tourism

A successful example of involving the wider community in tourism has been achieved at Lyndoch in South Australia. More than 70 per cent of businesses in Lyndoch ("the Gateway to the Barossa") have completed the AussieHost Business training program. The program has a tourism and customer-service focus, which emphasises that all businesses in a community are involved in tourism, either directly or indirectly.

More than two-thirds of the staff from businesses as varied as Australia Post, Patsy Biscoe Music Entertainment, Lyndoch Deli, Lyndoch Motors, Lyndoch Valley Meats, Mechanical Music Museum, Burge Family Wines, Lavender Farm, Country Cottage Bed and Breakfast, Kies Estate Wines, Christobelle Cottage, Glenfield Bed and Breakfast and the ANZ Bank have all been trained in the AussieHost program.

The aim of the program is to focus on interpersonal communication, customer relations and customer service with a focus on the tourism industry. It is a community-based one day program using trainers from the local community.

By encouraging the entire community to undertake the program, everyone is made aware of the importance of tourism to their area as well as receiving basic customer service training. A strong community network has grown between the AussieHost businesses, providing focus and direction, which in turn enables them to offer more to tourists.

As a consequence of this increased awareness and participation, the community will be more active and supportive of appropriate developments.

Many local groups, such as scouts and schools, may be interested in utilising the facilities or program of the tourism development once it is finished (taking tours or holding special events at the site). These same groups could also provide a small, eager workforce to assist in the research and development of the project.

Involving young people helps ensure support for the future of the business, and involving senior citizens, whose knowledge of the local area and its history can be invaluable, will broaden the support base further. Personal anecdotes from local residents can add "colour" to the product, and for many tourists, getting this additional information that they would not have found themselves is a major reason for taking a tour. If there is a university or TAFE campus in the region with an environmental science (or tourism/hospitality) school, linking in with these courses will provide you with further information on the environment and tourism opportunities, with the possibility of current and past students becoming potential guides.

As many non-residents may also have a stake in the area, they must also be consulted. This may be achieved by holding workshops in major cities, contacting various clubs and conservation groups or providing other opportunities for them to become involved when they are in the area (usually at peak tourist times).

Tourism operators can also gain community support by themselves supporting the local community, "giving something back", for example by supporting local conservation initiatives.

Supporting Conservation and the Local Community

Dolphin Encounters in Kaikora, New Zealand supports the local community recycling scheme by being on the trust that manages the recycling plant and contributing financially to specific projects, such as the purchase of large "wheely bins" for businesses in the town.

The company also supports local initiatives such as "Sea Week", and donates money for the purchase of related environmental books for local school libraries.

Dolphin Encounters contributes to ongoing research of marine mammals in the Southern Ocean by donating five dollars the sale of T-shirts to the Kaikora Dusky Dolphin Project, New Zealand What and Dolphin Trust and other related groups.

Difficulties in Community Participation

So, you have arranged a series of meetings to involve the community, but no-one turns up. Taking this as a sign of lack of interest, you continue with your tourism plans, only to face a massive community backlash once you have established your business and started bringing in tourists. You may even end up in court, defending your business operations.

Community apathy can be a major problem, but it is important to persevere, and often by incorporating educational institutions, you may eventually get the whole family involved. Another problem is that the more vocal elements may gain the upper hand, with the silent majority not moving until it is too late.

To minimise these problems, you must make an effort to ensure community consultation has been adequate. Personal contact with the leaders of local community groups who may be affected by the tourism development (including tours and activities), and offering to speak to a meeting of the group is an essential first step. Even if the group does not show great interest, keep them informed through newsletters or other correspondence. Joining some of these groups and attending meetings will provide evidence of your commitment to the issues they regard as important. This is especially the case with local conservation groups that may be interested in one very local issue such as the protection of an endangered butterfly or tree.

EcoNetwork Combines Skills

Port Stephens, on the New South Wales coast, has experienced dramatic growth in popularity as both a tourist destination and a place to live. This resulted in rapid growth during the 1980s and 1990s, with sections of the community becoming concerned by the pro-development policy of the local council.

Until 1990, community relationships in the development and tourism areas were in a state of chaos, with little communication between the various stakeholders. Development plans were presented for "community consultation" with little or no time to respond. The local council and developers and the various community groups were seen as adversaries. Communication was confrontational and each group displayed little concern for the others.

In an effort to improve the situation, some of the community groups organised a one day conference towards the end of 1991. The Council President and local State Member for Parliament attended along with community conservation groups and pro-development interests. It became clear from discussions that the natural and heritage assets of the region could be utilised to meet the diverse needs of the community groups, while giving incentives to promote "appropriate" developments and increased tourism.

A new organisation called EcoNetwork-Port Stephens comprising 17 community groups was formed. By bringing the groups together, the skills of many committed people are now used in a constructive way. Ideas on projects and policies are fed into the community through the network, with time and opportunity for feedback and identification of any potential problems.

Benefits gained from establishment of the EcoNetwork include improved communications and organisational relationships, sharing of expertise and resources, and integration of the decision-making process.

Most importantly, the network was developed and put to work immediately as a result of the initial conference. It is crucial that such conferences, workshops or meetings are not seen as merely "talk-fests", but that they actually achieve some outcomes and that the local community is made aware of them.

Local media (newspapers, radio and television) can be a great tool for disseminating information and raising discussion in the community. They are always looking for good stories and issues, and tourism development is one that often grabs their interest. The media can also be used as an extremely cost-effective marketing tool (see Chapter 6).

One way to make ensure that you include all the various stakeholders and interest groups is to contact your local government, who should be familiar with all the main groups in the community.

Local Government

Local councils are directly and indirectly involved in tourism, providing much of the necessary public infrastructure and services, such as airports, bus terminals, convention centres, art centres, sidewalk cafes, museums, visitor information centres, community recreation centres, public toilets, rubbish collection, street cleaning, public gardens and parks, and signage.

Councils are also involved in decisions about the types of activities that are permitted in public places; for example, some towns, in an effort to reduce vandalism and general "loutish" behaviour that may affect the community and tourists, have areas where alcohol consumption is not permitted. Councils support cultural festivals and special events, and many have developed international relationships with sister cities and youth exchange programs — potential tourist markets.

Due to the broad-ranging interest in tourism, and its close relationship with the community, the elected representatives (local councillors) and their staff are in a good position to help tourism operators in their dealings with the local community. Some have already taken the lead in negotiations between different players, acting as mediator and facilitator in many discussions, and allowing tourism to co-exist with other industries.

Planning Tourist Accommodation

Busselton Shire in Western Australia has two major tourist attractions — an established wine industry and beautiful beaches. The wine industry was wary of any focussed tourism promotion, expressing concern about how extra tourists would be accommodated and, like other residents, wanting to maintain the rural character of the area.

The council took the initiative and brought together all the stakeholders to formulate a Rural Tourist Accommodation Policy which would establish the framework for any further development, be it in tourism or agriculture.

After two years of negotiation and consultation, broad consensus was achieved and a policy established that the community owned. As well as the strategy, the council now has a process for working through tourism-related issues with the community, which will continue to be of benefit in the future.

Virtually all areas that local government is involved in have an impact on tourism, so councils need to develop tourism policies that integrate the needs of the tourism industry and the community with the priorities of the council. The areas that local governments control in relation to tourism can be divided into the following general groups:

Planning
Local government, usually through a council-funded tourist association, makes decisions on tourism planning and strategy development for the area. These plans, or tourism strategies, generally investigate the need for coordinated decision-making processes and provide a vision for the area, which forms the basis for many planning decisions, covering economic, environmental and social factors.

Controls
Local governments make many of the decisions on the development of tourism guidelines and controls, such as permission to operate sidewalk cafes, outdoor theatre and permits to serve alcohol.

Land Use
Decisions on land use in relation to tourism enterprises, such as the zoning or re-zoning of categories of permissible development, are part of local council's responsibilities. This is an extremely important aspect affecting tourism development and even activities on private land.

Infrastructure
Local governments make decisions on the development of tourism infrastructure and amenities, such as visitor information centres, information boards, signage and public toilet facilities. They also prioritise and manage road-works and the maintenance of public infrastructure.

Development
The council considers and approves major tourism development proposals, based on whether they are in line with the tourism plan/strategy, council regulations and legislation, as well as considering the environmental, economic and social impacts of the development.

Information and Cooperation
The council determines the direction and extent of tourism promotion, tourist information services, regional cooperation and economic development. This is usually outlined in the Tourism Strategy.

Impacts

An increasingly important role of local government is to consider the impacts and implications of tourism in general, as well as individual enterprises and developments.

Funding

The council makes numerous funding decisions for the tourism-oriented aspects of its business, such as funding the local/regional tourism association, visitor information centre, special projects and research.

Influences on Council Decision-Making

It is important to recognise the complexities of the decisions that local councillors are required to make, even in just one area such as tourism. Being aware of the many factors that can influence this decision-making process, may assist tourism operators to recognise the main forces at play on a particular decision.

No matter how impartial councillors may be, they are still human and will be influenced to some extent by their background and personal values or interests. It is often these values and interests that encouraged the community to elect them in the first place.

A major influence on councillors is their own sense of responsibility to improve the quality of life for all members of the community. Those observing council behaviour may consider this "big picture" view to be misguided at times by, but it undoubtedly has a strong influence on many council decisions. Direction from the council's mission or plan and legal or regulatory requirements will also influence councillors' decisions.

Another influence is persuasion from internal or external sources, such as other councillors, administration staff, special advisers, the media, and community groups, including tourism operators. Many councillors will seek the advice of others, particularly if they are not familiar with the issues involved, so often those who are most easily accessible (or available) to them can have a great impact.

This leads to the issue of access of relevant information — the quality of information can be poor, or there may just be too much of it. Attempting to gain a complete set of information about all the alternatives concerning a particular issue can result in an overload of information that becomes unwieldy and virtually impossible to deal with. However, if decision-making is done selectively, using a limited range of the available information, there is a high risk of bias and oversimplification of the issues and their impacts. Information overload is a major problem facing councillors, and as a consequence they will often turn to advisers (official or unofficial).

So, when working with the local council, it is important to be aware of all these influences, and to use them.

Bike Trail Gets Community & Council Support

The Howitt Bicycle Trail — An East Gippsland Experience! is a 750 kilometre bicycle trail through eastern Victoria. The project was funded from the Sidney Myer Fund, which was impressed with the high level of municipal and community support for the project. The Gippsland Regional Development Board initiated the project, and gained support from the eight municipalities crossed by the trail, Bicycle Victoria, Tourism Victoria, and the Municipal Association of Victoria's Community Jobs Innovation Grant Scheme. A local cyclist designed the route, and training opportunities were provided for local people working alongside the tradespeople.

One of the benefits of developing the trail was that tourists were channelled to small towns off the main highway, thus increasing the return to local communities. This cooperative effort enabled a relatively low cost, low-impact tourist product to be developed, which benefited many areas of the community.

How to Approach Local Council

Different groups in the community, such as local traders and council staff, may have different goals. The local traders will be most interested in finding out how an enterprise will affect them — for example, how many extra steaks the butcher will sell once your tours are operating. The language and approach used here should be direct and relevant to the individual, and can be easily done face-to-face.

Local council's information needs are very different, often requiring a more structured approach. A well worded letter that includes relevant information will get a response from the council.

All correspondence goes to the desk of the chief executive officer, regardless of who it is addressed to, so address your proposal to the CEO who will then pass it on to the appropriate person/department. Word your letter so that it requires a response, either by requesting a reply, or by asking that it be listed in council for their consideration, which is even more effective. If your proposal requires some funding or resourcing from the council (such as improving access to your property), a request for confirmation from council that the proposal will be considered in the budget at the next meeting should also elicit a response.

This next point should be obvious, but it is important — always be polite, both by letter, on the phone and face-to-face. Council staff are human, and will not react well to a rude, demanding attitude (whether it is justified or not). If the council made a promise to do something that has not been attended to, remind them politely and include a copy of the letter that the promise was made in — a main reason for obtaining a written response to any request you make.

Local government is becoming more and more budget-conscious, so any proposal or request you make that will cost them must clearly demonstrate economic and social benefits. For example, if you are requesting a recycling program to be established for the waste from your ecotourism venture, point out the benefits such as reduction of land-fill, a cleaner local environment etc. Also indicate in-kind community or personal support that is available, such as a local worm-farmer offering to collect the newspapers for his farm, another providing collection points on various properties, locals prepared to distribute information on the program etc. This not only provides a direct economic benefit to the council, but also displays social benefits of increasing civic pride through community support.

This community support is important, and any letters of endorsement should be included with your proposal. In this instance, "community" may mean your neighbours or people in your street, the tourism industry, or suppliers, depending on the nature of the proposal. By getting a group of supporters together, your proposal will have a greater impact. Do not be afraid of opposition — by identifying those groups who may oppose your proposal and showing that you are communicating with them, you show the council that you are considering all aspects.

Finally, have alternative plans, so that if your first proposal is rejected, you can come straight back with another, modified concept.

Regardless of whom you are dealing with, try and look at the situation from their point of view so you can highlight "what's in it for them". This will increase your chance of success.

Indigenous Communities

Incorporating aspects of indigenous culture into your tourist product can be an extremely enjoyable, educational and satisfying experience for your guests. As ecotourists are interested in the environment and local communities, they welcome contact with a culture that has lived with the land for thousands of years. Many Maori and Aboriginal communities see ecotourism as an appropriate form of tourism for them as it respects and protects their environment. Also, many see tourism as a way of increasing the understanding between cultures and promoting reconciliation.

Most parts of Australia and New Zealand have an indigenous community associated with them, even if it is small and displaced, as in much of southern Australia. It is important to locate the local indigenous community and develop a relationship with them if you want to incorporate some aspects of Aboriginal life in your operation. The local council and tourism association should be able to provide contacts for the relevant local communities.

Indigenous Culture Provides a Unique Experience

In 1988, members of an Aboriginal family at Angatja, near the Northern Territory–South Australia border, approached some non-Aboriginal friends to form a joint business, "Desert Tracks". The Aboriginal family provided the destination, itinerary and traditional teaching, whilst their non-Aboriginal partners raised the funds for equipment, marketing and staff. The Aborigines had to meet the requirements of their own community (the Anangu Pitjantjatjara) to get permits from them to operate their tours. They worked through this process by talking at meetings and taking observers from the Council on their trips.

The business is keeping alive the law and culture of this indigenous community as well as conserving the environment. It is also providing skilled work for their families as guides, interpreters, drivers, cooks and office staff, with the company now being run solely by the Aboriginal community.

In order to maintain the integrity of the environment as well as their culture, the company has a limit of 200 visitors per year, which provides them with a small profit.

Tourism operators and indigenous communities cooperate to varying degrees, depending on the nature of the community and its elders. Some do not feel that non-indigenous people should be permitted to discuss any aspects of their lifestyle, such as the Aboriginal Dreamtime. Whereas others are more lenient and agree that if you are asked a question by a tourist, you should answer it to the best of your ability, regardless of your background. Finding out the attitudes of the community you will be dealing with before meeting them will save much time and effort in the long term. Local council or other tour operators should be able to provide this information.

In order to be truly effective, consultation must be a two-way process, and Aboriginal groups should consider the needs of the non-indigenous communities or groups when dealing with them. As tourism can benefit all groups, this cooperation will ensure that everyone has an equal opportunity to benefit.

Protocol and Decision-Making Dynamics

When dealing with indigenous communities, it is important to understand their structure and decision-making processes. Aboriginal communities generally operate on a consensus that is overseen by the elders. Like working with any community, the consultation and discussion process can take time, even years, to reach a conclusion. Non-indigenous people who arrive, expecting to run their tours to sacred sites in a few months time, are quickly brought to earth by these communities — they would be lucky to have had any contact with the elders in that time, let alone come to a working relationship.

Mootwingee: Working with the Aboriginal Community

Mootwingee National Park, near Broken Hill in south-western New South Wales has, in recent years, worked closely with its local indigenous community.

An unsuccessful land claim by the Mutawintji Local Aboriginal Land Council (MLALC) for the Mootwingee Historic Site highlighted the severely degraded condition of many of the Aboriginal relics. As a result, the NSW Premier instigated a plan of management for the site. The plan was developed in consultation with the MLALC and adopted in 1989.

It included guidelines to protect the cultural integrity of the area, with access limited to those in the company of National Parks staff, a MLALC member or accredited guide. Inappropriate walking trails were removed and others created; and the visitor information centre was to be redeveloped as a Mutawintji Centre that would tell the Aboriginal story of Mootwingee.

In 1991 the freehold title of Mootwingee was handed back to the local Aboriginal community, based on the Uluru and Kakadu models, with the MLALC leasing back the land to the government for a minimum of 30 years.

Also in that year, the first annual tour guide school was held at the park. It is offered to both Aboriginal and non-Aboriginal people, and accredits guides on an annual basis. In 1995 an Aboriginal heritage tourism project officer was employed, and in 1996 an Aboriginal tourism liaison officer was also employed to help facilitate the creation of Mutawintji Tours. It is intended that the new company will provide trained Aboriginal guides for all activities in the park.

Consultation between non-Aboriginal tour operators and the Aboriginal community is proving successful. The community approached the non-Aboriginal guides to determine their interest in sub-contracting an Aboriginal guide on their tours. Most of the tour operators agreed that an Aboriginal guide would be preferable, even though they had been trained and were accredited to guide the tours themselves.

Different people have a different sense of time — farmers do not move at the same pace as city people, and most indigenous communities have their own concept of time and its importance. Do not rush your planning, negotiations, or tours, remember that this different attitude to time is often what appeals to tourists.

Camp Coorong

The Ngarrindjeri community developed Camp Coorong, in South Australia with a vision of beginning the process of reconciliation by teaching the cultural history of the area. Initially developed in 1987 for school children, Camp Coorong has hosted tour groups from overseas as well as interstate, and plans to develop an ecotourism program.

Decision-making and management is run cooperatively. The local community runs Camp Coorong through a committee that refers all major issues back to the whole community (about 100 people).

New Zealand Maoris must be treated according to their status under the Treaty of Waitangi, the Resource management Act and other relevant legislation. They must not be considered as a minority interest group. It is crucial that they are consulted early and that you are familiar with their protocol and decision-making dynamics. All relevant tribes must be identified and then a cooperative agreement reached to establish the tribe that has tangata whenua status over the area.

It is critical that your discussion with tangata whenua (and Aboriginal elders), starts with issues, not a development proposal, as a proposal suggests that you have already considered the issues and made your decisions.

Silence does not indicate approval, and if you have no response from the indigenous leaders it may be that they have had insufficient time to consider the issues or that they have had bad experiences in the past. Look for alternative approaches and continue consultation until you have a response.

The number of tourism businesses being established by Maoris in New Zealand and Aborigines in Australia is increasing, enabling them to become more independent and self-sufficient. A number of case studies, including the ones mentioned here, show how successful they can be in developing tourism, and increasing cultural pride.

Tourism and Cultural Identity

At Wallace Rockhole, an Aboriginal town near Alice Springs, tourism has helped preserve the community's cultural identity by providing an outlet and market for their arts and jobs for their youth. Tourism has been the catalyst for preservation of indigenous knowledge through bush tucker and rock art tours. The number of tourists is limited and their behaviour controlled through the tours.

Another benefit of community-based tourism enterprises is the re-education of visitors in their attitudes towards Aboriginal groups — the town is a successful example of a community operating with pride and moving towards self-sufficiency.

The local council makes decisions only after consulting with (and gaining approval from) community elders. This ensures widespread community support for the town's tourism industry.

The Pitfalls of Indigenous Tourism

Tourism has many positive benefits for all those involved, but it also has negative aspects, not only environmentally, but also socially. This is particularly true of indigenous cultures, which tend to be more sensitive to tourism than some other cultures.

When something of great intrinsic worth is turned into a commodity it can lose some of its original value. This is true for tourism which can alter the nature of what it is selling, particularly from a social point of view. History can become sanitised and generalised, and there are many cases where this has occurred with Maori and Australian Aboriginal tourism. For example, tourists expect to see an Aborigine playing the didgeridoo wherever they are in Australia, even though it was not a traditional instrument in southern areas. Despite this, few tourism enterprises in southern Australia do not incorporate didgeridoo playing and sell the instruments.

When two cultures, such as the host (indigenous culture) and the guest (usually western or Asian), come together, exchange of ideas will occur. This is one of the benefits of tourism, providing an opportunity to break down barriers and perceptions, but there is a negative aspect of cultural exchange. Often, one culture will dominate the other. For example, the guests' holiday culture, incorporating disposable cash, relaxation and indolence may make the hosts wish to experience a similar lifestyle, and create false expectations and demands in the indigenous community. Resentment may also be generated by the fact that those in the indigenous community cannot access the same lifestyle as their guests, resulting in an increase in petty crimes against the tourists.

Privacy is another major issue for all communities, but particularly relevant to indigenous communities as they are much smaller and contained than most other local communities. Tourists in general, and ecotourists in particular, are interested in learning about, meeting and interacting with the indigenous community in a manner that they believe to be authentic — they want to be welcomed into these communities as an "equal". Many communities find this desire incompatible with their need for privacy, particularly in their own homes and during religious rites and ceremonies. Visitors to the community that lives near Uluru were banned after a current affairs television reporter barged into their homes unannounced with television cameras running. This type of insensitive approach causes great distress and harms the whole tourism industry. Even though this incident was not directly tourism related, the consequences have been felt most by the tourism industry.

Of course, not all indigenous communities will have enough members with the right sort of people skills required for tourism, so they will need to import people with the skills and expertise. Bringing in "outsiders" will create friction and resentment in the local community, and most Maoris and Aborigines are reluctant to enter another community's land.

The stress on resources can also cause social conflict. For example, the need for additional (or a different type of) sewage and waste treatment, litter control and the destruction or alteration of scenic attributes, which often have a sacred significance, can create resentment towards tourists and operators. Indigenous communities have a close relationship with the land and take a long-term approach to its management — something many western cultures are just starting to recognise — and so they are sensitive to land degradation from both practical and spiritual aspects.

How can we ensure these social issues do not become insurmountable barriers to ecotourism? Through REAL community consultation and participation, not just lip service. The local social framework needs to be recognised and catered to before tourist needs.

Special Note:

To be relevant to all of Australia and New Zealand, this section has purposely been presented extremely generally, as there are major differences between the tribes. It is important to discuss local conditions with the appropriate council and indigenous representatives to ascertain the specific nature of the communities you wish to deal with.

Ecotourism and Culture

Culture and heritage, both indigenous and non-indigenous, are integral parts of the natural landscape, and as such are also a part of ecotourism. The definition of ecotourism by the Ecotourism Association of Australia presented in Chapter One refers to fostering "environmental and cultural understanding (and) appreciation…".

Combining Environmental and Cultural Heritage

O'Reilly's Guest House in the Lamington National Park in southern Queensland attracts guests by its combination of environmental beauty and pioneering heritage.

In 1911, the O'Reilly family selected 200 hectares of rainforest west of the Gold Coast to start a dairy farm. When the Lamington National Park was proclaimed, it surrounded the O'Reilly farm on all sides, cutting them off from their markets as the only road was a perilous pack-horse trail. A constant flow of scientists, naturalists and other visitors to the park suggested an alternative for the family and in 1926 they opened their guest house.

The O'Reillys gained international fame in 1937 when Bernard O'Reilly found the wreckage of the Stinson Airliner VH-UHH with two survivors, 11 days after the plane crashed in rugged country. O'Reilly was convinced that searchers were looking for the plane in the wrong area, so he set off on his own, found the wreck and saved the two survivors in dramatic circumstances. Much publicity was given to the bushcraft and the hardy spirit of Australia's pioneers. The heritage of the O'Reilly family is truly rich and guests still want to learn of those early times.

The guest house operates as an ecotourism enterprise with guided walks, information and activities, as well as providing evidence of a living pioneer heritage with ten family members actively involved in the business.

Special Events — the Ultimate Community Tourism Activity

A special event or festival can involve whole towns and communities, both as organisers and participants. Hundreds of festivals are run throughout Australia, some with an environmental theme. Ecotourism should be an integral part of these — if not the reason for the festival in the first place. Festivals can generate civic pride, increase visitors to a region, add value to a visitor's stay or to an ecotourism product by being incorporated into a tour, attraction or accommodation package, and raise the quality of a visitor's experience.

A town or community can enhance its reputation by holding a festival, particularly an environmentally based one, which reflects a widespread commitment to the environment. Special events often provide the opportunity to create spin-off attractions that may extend the period of interest in the town/community.

Special events, such as festivals, due to their size and the involvement of a large number of community groups, are excellent examples of community cooperation. While the event itself provides great opportunities for a community, the community or town also provides opportunities for the event, from creating both local and global networks through sister-city relationships, to increasing attendance numbers and raising the quality of the event. The town and its networks can provide greater exposure for sponsorship — an important component of any event — providing additional benefits and enticements for the sponsorship dollar.

Strategies to Develop a Special Event

One of the most important considerations when developing a special event is to create a consistent theme. This may include a corporate logo and umbrella branding, such as the Australian Formula 1 Grand Prix which has its own colour scheme and features the chequered flag. Approved merchandise is sold to shops and restaurants for their displays, maintaining a strong overall corporate image. The Wangaratta Jazz and Blues Festival features black and white designs throughout the town and in shop windows; towns on the rodeo circuit promote these events by focusing on cowboy imagery.

Some examples of an ecotourism style special event could include environmental days with ecotour activities and attractions, land care events, local indigenous and other community heritage festivals, alternative energy and waste minimisation events, and innovative construction for farms and homes. Even some "new age" style festivals and many other festivals could incorporate elements of the environment and ecotourism activities.

When developing a special event it is important to establish good information forums where the whole community (as well as the neighbouring ones) are kept informed and given opportunities to participate. This can be done through newspaper articles, newsletters, event updates posted around town, talks to clubs and associations and at public meetings. The needs of each group must be understood, particularly those of local businesses and residents, and this will open happen through communication and consultation. For example, residents may be concerned about restrictions to parking on the weekend of the event, so they may need to be encouraged to shop during the week to limit their inconvenience.

Some businesses will find that they lose patrons during a festival, including some who may be expecting to gain. For example, some restaurants near the Grand Prix circuit in Adelaide found that their regular customers stayed away because of crowds and parking difficulties. After they paid for extra late licences and staff overtime they were no better off than without the Grand Prix. However, they did not consider the ongoing benefit of their higher profile to more people who will visit the area and its restaurants throughout the year. This is a major benefit of an event (particularly in rural areas), and one that is also extremely hard to quantify — the ongoing benefit of greater exposure. People who visit a town for a special event are often encouraged to return to experience more of what the region has to offer. This element of exposure should be maximised as much as possible and businesses made aware of its power.

Another benefit to the local community that should be stressed is the development of infrastructure that may be needed to hold the event - these public facilities will be there for the whole community to use and enjoy throughout the year.

Another important element in the planning of an event is the development of a promotional strategy. Close attention should be paid to cooperative benefits and promotion throughout the community and beyond. For example, local businesses could include a brochure or newsletter on the event with their monthly accounts, local tour operators and accommodation providers offering special packages and promotional tours. Travelling sales representatives can also be great promoters of an event, particularly if they see it as an opportunity to sell more of their product (cleaning supplies, toilet paper, etc.).

Networking

The tourism industry is a people industry — your product is developed for people (the tourists) — and as such good relationships with others in the industry and related areas are pivotal to your success. By belonging to local community groups, speaking at functions, offering your services in fund-raising enterprises you not only create a positive profile of yourself and your business, but also make many valuable contacts and friends. Many tourism operators are generous in their assistance, offering great advice on the pitfalls and hazards that they encountered as well as positive support. Most successful operators recognise the benefit to them in increasing tourism in general to their area, and do not look on other tourism businesses as direct competitors. You will often find them speaking at seminars and workshops, providing invaluable practical experience and assistance.

When looking for good tourism networks, the best place to start is with your local or regional tourism association. These groups are able to tap into the resources of national organisations such as the Australian Tourist Commission, the Bureau of Tourism Research, and the federal Office of National Tourism. They can keep you informed about any marketing/promotional opportunities, new tourism data that may relate to your business and conferences and publications that could help you. Your local association should also be able to link you with any relevant industry associations that you should consider joining, such as the Ecotourism Association of Australia (EAA).

The EAA is a national group that provides networking and assistance in the environmental aspects of tourism, in particular ecotourism. It may also be worth joining a state or local tourism group. Once again, your tourism association should be able to advise you, or at the very least, put you in touch with people who can give you more information. If they do not have this information, speak to other successful tourism operators.

Many associations offer their members a range of benefits, from discount accommodation and services of other members, to group purchasing benefits such as insurance, fuel, training, and telephone. Some associations require their members to be accredited by them or to adhere to a code of conduct to receive a full member status, whilst others request a level of training or years of tourism experience for each level of membership, and some merely require the payment of a joining fee.

Appendix Three contains contact details for the ecotourism and general tourism industry. The list is fairly comprehensive, but may not contain all the smaller, regional groups or associations.

Conclusion

The community is made up of different people with different needs, who must be kept informed and feel that they have some ownership of tourism in their area. Involve young people but do not neglect the expertise and knowledge of the older residents who can add value to your product.

Councils require a conscientious effort, and are primarily interested in the economic and social benefits of any proposal. Gaining community support and assistance will increase the probability of the proposal being approved.

Find out who and where your local indigenous community is, and involve them wherever it is possible and practical.

Networking with local tourism groups and operators will provide you with a great deal of support and information as well as help to further align you with the local community.

By showing how each group will gain from your enterprise and listening to their concerns and needs, support and success should follow.

Cooperation Leads to New Ecotourism Development

A project that changed significantly from its original concept after consultation with the local community is the development of the Tilligerry Habitat at Port Stephens.

A proposal for a caravan park development on the Tilligerry Peninsula raised community concern about the conservation value of the Peninsula as a koala corridor. A local conservation group presented an alternative proposal which included the development of an ecotourism interpretive centre. Community involvement in on-site rehabilitation, to restore land severely degraded by sand mining, was recommended as part of the project. The revenue-raising ecotourism aspect was designed to fund the rehabilitation works, providing an environmental and economic resource for the community as a whole.

Students at the University of Newcastle have become involved in defining the impacts on residents in relation to who may profit from the venture, and a New Work Opportunities grant provided funding to train and employ tour guides.

This is a good example of developing partnerships between the community, conservation groups and developers.

4 Working in the Environment

Many activities are undertaken outdoors in either an active or passive form, from adventure activities such as rock climbing, rafting and horse riding through to bushwalking, camping, photography, bird watching and looking at wildflowers. They can all be incorporated into an ecotour, and all have a potential impact on the environment depending on their level of intensity and location. Sustainable practices within these activities are as important as those in building and construction covered in the next chapter.

Managing the Resource

Many ecotourism operations utilise public land that is managed by either local, state or federal governments. The issues encountered by these land managers are often the same as on private property. An understanding of the issues of land management and tourism is essential to operating in the outdoor environment on both public and private land.

Carrying Capacity

All farmers are familiar with the term, carrying capacity, as used to express the number of units of production that can be sustained on a certain area of land, for example, heads of sheep per hectare. Carrying capacity in tourism terms is used to indicate the number of people that a site can cope with before it deteriorates. But, as so often happens when terms are taken from one field and used in another, it does not quite fit.

As well as the number of people, many other variables have an impact on the environment, such as the behaviour of visitors, weather and rainfall conditions, where the site is situated (near main roads or in a remote national park), and the length of stay of visitors. Also, different groups have vastly different opinions about the level of environmental impact that is acceptable.

Carrying capacity in tourism should consider social and psychological factors as well as physical and biological ones. It is in this socio-psychological area that many diverse opinions exist. Bushwalkers who travel to remote areas singly or in pairs may resent the presence of other groups. They would probably consider a tour group at their camp-site to be invading their sense of adventure and solitude, whereas other walkers may enjoy the social interaction with other groups. Generally speaking, the further removed people are from access points and roads, the less tolerant they are of sharing sites and trails with others.

Any definition of carrying capacity in relation to tourism would need to refer to the amount of people that a site can carry without unacceptable change in the quality of the environment and the quality of the experience. Each person in the discussion may have a different perception of what this means.

Don't Misinterpret the Signs

At the Jenolan Caves in New South Wales, there was concern that the increasing number of tourists would cause irreversible impacts on the environment of the caves. With visitor numbers at 260,00 per annum, and increasing by about five per cent, a study was initiated to determine the carrying capacity of the caves.

Visitor movements were monitored and environmental indicators observed, with some interesting results. Some of the erosion on tracks that was initially thought to be due to the numbers of visitors was actually the result of poor planning and siting — erosion was occurring regardless of the number of people on the track.

Some of the environmental indicators that were chosen were not appropriate, as readings of the water levels in the cave were affected by climatic shifts as well as tourist numbers.

These two examples, where the impact of tourist numbers was potentially misinterpreted, illustrate the importance of identifying all the reasons for environmental (and social) degradation, not just the expected one.

Minimising Environmental and Social Conflicts

It is important to understand some of the processes used by land managers to "control" the activities, behaviour and numbers of visitors to sensitive areas. Measures to increase carrying capacity (and/or decrease usage) include a range of options covered by three basic categories: site management, direct regulation, and indirect regulation. These are the basic tools of land management.

Site Management
Harden Site
Some of the ways in which a site can be hardened can be relatively non-intrusive, whereas areas that could be highly impacted and have a large

number of people using them are often hardened by fairly intrusive methods. These methods (from least to most intrusive) include thinning the ground cover and overstory, converting to more hardy plant species, irrigating or draining, revegetating or installing durable surfaces. This can include building boardwalks, walkways and bridges.

Channel Use

Visitor use can be channelled by erecting barriers (rocks, logs, fences), constructing paths, closing tracks or utilising the natural landscape. However, sending people to other areas could compound the problem of environmental degradation and track closures may not always be successful due to the generally slow rate of revegetation and poor compliance by users. Education on correct behaviour (such as remaining on designated tracks) provided by responsible ecotour operators can improve the situation significantly.

Educating Visitors Protects Ancient Marine Life

Marine stromatolites, identical to the earliest forms of life found in fossil records, are formed by micro-organisms building mushroom shaped structures up to one-metre high. Hamelin Pool, in Shark Bay, Western Australia is one of only two sites in the world where marine stromatolites live.

The area has been easily accessible, and much damage has been done to the site by visitors walking over the stromatolites, often unaware of their significance. A boardwalk was proposed to limit the damage and control visitor access and movement. The nature of stromatolites and their marine environment required some innovation in relation to design and construction.

As the micro-organisms that colonise to form the structures need light for growth, the gauge and placement of the decking of the boardwalk had to be arranged so that sufficient light could pass through to the organisms while maintaining visitor safety. Traditional chemical treatments used to preserve wood in marine environments could not be used because of the risk to the micro-organisms, so non-chemically treated jarrah wood was used.

Being shallow and tidal, the site is exposed to the air for much of the time, and the lack of surrounding vegetation to screen it and provide natural entry points to the site, created a challenge to keep visitors on the official tracks and boardwalks. With the introduction of interpretative and educational material that highlights the importance of the site and the need to keep to the designated pathways, visitors are staying on the tracks and boardwalk.

Develop Facilities

Facilities that provide access to currently under-used areas, provision of toilet blocks, accommodation, interpretation facilities or camping areas, barbeques and picnic grounds all help to encourage use of an area. In this way, areas of congregation (such as picnic grounds) can be managed and hardened to handle the impacts of numbers of people, leaving other areas undisturbed. The term "sacrifice zone" is sometimes used for such areas.

Boardwalk in the Valley of the Giants

The Valley of the Giants in south-west Western Australia is a forest that contains the unique red tingle tree and Gondwana invertebrate relics The trees, which are many hundreds of years old, have the biggest diameter trunk of any eucalypt.

The popular site, which had over 140,000 visitors in 1991, was suffering from the impact of all these people. A maze of tracks led to the trees, which were trampled around their bases by the visitors, compacting the soil and damaging the trees' shallow root systems. The level of visitation was also disturbing the leaf litter that is the habitat of some unique Gondwana invertebrates.

A series of boardwalks has been developed, including a Tree Tops walk and the Ancient Empire Boardwalk. The walks are curved to harmonise with the surrounds and enhance the visitor's sense of discovery as they are drawn around each bend. Interpretive signs are included, and contemplative rest points and lookout platforms have been strategically placed, utilising the natural vegetation.

The boardwalks succeed in keeping visitors off the forest floor and provide additional interpretation and understanding of the site, creating new tourist experiences. Commercial tours may utilise this attraction and help to pay for park management through their permit fees.

Direct Regulation
Increase Enforcement
Enforcement agencies have the option of imposing fines for non-compliance or increasing surveillance. The latter is not practical in most national parks and reserves of Australia and New Zealand due to their size, number of entry points and lack of available staff. Private land-owners should be able (in most cases) to enforce compliance by granting or refusing permission to access the property.

Zone Use
Zoning spatially (eg areas for walkers only), or for uses over time (such as summer months only) and limiting camping stop-overs to one night at each site have some limiting effect on usage, numbers and damage. Zoning is a popular form of regulation used by many public land managers with varying degrees of effectiveness — once again it needs to be monitored, which is not always possible due to staffing limitations.

Restrict Activities
Restricting activities such as the building of campfires and limiting activities such as fishing or hunting are also options that land managers use. In many

areas overnight camping must be at designated sites (particularly for tour groups) and the use of dead wood, which provides homes for small mammals and insects as well as nourishing the soil through decomposition, is not permitted for fires.

Restrict Intensity of Use

Rotating the use of an area by opening and closing access roads, requiring reservations for campsites, assigning camps, and limiting group sizes and length of stay are options available to managers attempting to restrict the intensity of use of an area, which are used extensively in Australia and New Zealand. Some of these restrictions can create problems for tour operators as they must have alternative arrangements if sites or access roads are closed without warning. Also, planning itineraries up to two years in advance (as is necessary for marketing and promotion purposes, particularly to the overseas market) can be difficult if popular campsites cannot be reserved so far ahead.

Permits

Issuing permits is another direct way of regulating resource use, and is required for most commercial operators on public land, including logging contractors, apiarists and miners, as well as tourism operators.

Ration Cards

The use of "ration cards", although not common practice, has some merit and is being used in other environmental areas. The idea is to issue cards with a certain number of points which are used each time you visit an area. Popular and intensively used sites would require more points than visits to less heavily used areas. This would encourage users to select less popular areas, but it might just shift the problems to those areas, so the system would need to be monitored.

Indirect Regulation

Many people consider direct control to be too heavy-handed as the main method of land use regulation. The challenge for environmental land management lies in the development and implementation of indirect controls that can delay and minimise the imposition of direct controls.

Pricing Strategies

Fees can be charged as a fixed entrance fee or differential fees by the trail, zone, or season. Fees can limit, encourage or transfer use from one site to another. Commercial operations on public land are required to pay a fee for the opportunity to make money from the use of public land (such as one dollar

The Kangaroo Island Sea Lions

Seal Bay Conservation Park on Kangaroo Island, South Australia is a major breeding ground for the rare Australian Sea Lion. These creatures were hunted to near-extinction with a remnant colony surviving at Seal Bay. Apart from visits by a few locals, the sea lions were left alone until the 1950s when a tour operator began taking groups to Seal Bay.

Because of concern about visitors interfering with the sea lions (who display no fear of humans and can be easily approached), two prohibited zones were declared where females could give birth and nurture their young undisturbed. However, other problems were caused by the visitor carpark near the beach, with its noise and pit toilets that trapped curious seal pups. The pups also often sought shade under parked cars, which increased their risk of being run over.

Visitor numbers grew steadily to reach about 20,000 in the mid 1970s. In the late 1970s the car park was moved to a site further from the beach, with a sealed track and boardwalk constructed over the dunes. Ranger supervision was implemented during peak periods.

Visitor numbers continued to grow rapidly, with 35,000 visitors in 1985, requiring additional strategies to ensure the protection of the sea lions and their habitat. Research showed that the sea lions were stressed by the close presence of so many humans, and there was a danger of a visitor being seriously attacked — a legal and ethical issue which the land managers did not wish to encounter. The aggressive reactions were being provoked by the increased number of visitors and a change in the type of tourist. Large numbers of international tourists were visiting (many of them unable to read the English language signs) who were less aware of the risks associated with being near wild animals.

The National Parks and Wildlife Service (NPWS) adopted a user pays guided tour system in which access to the colony was permitted only to fee-paying groups who were escorted either by trained NPWS officers or approved tour operators. The number of groups on the beach at any one time was also limited.

Locals were initially opposed to the restrictions as they believed they had a right to visit Seal Bay as they chose. Tourism operators were concerned that the requirements would result in fewer tourists to the bay and to Kangaroo Island. However, more than 80,000 people visited Seal Bay in 1993, and the fact that all funds generated are used in management projects on Kangaroo Island has helped to gain local support.

One indication of the success of the management strategy has been an increase in the number of female sea lions giving birth on the main beach, despite the presence of humans.

A viewing platform and alternative boardwalk have been built to cope with increased tourist traffic and to limit the incidence of erosion caused by foot traffic. The increased presence of guiding staff has reduced littering. A solar powered interpretation centre has been established at the entrance to the restricted zone, providing visitors with information on the sea lions and minimal impact behaviour.

This combination of management techniques from zoning to site hardening, channelling use, and education appears to be working successfully. Monitoring will continue as the park managers recognise that managing the environment is an ongoing process.

per person per day). Taxes on complementary goods (such as bed tax or food supplies) have been suggested as a means to raise further tourism-related revenue for public land management, but these are not effective as they are too indirect, and affect those not actually visiting the park.

Manipulation of Access and Infrastructure

An area can be made more remote by blocking off access roads to extend the length of the entry trip. This affects the number and type of people who visit, with only the more adventurous making the effort to reach these areas. Modification of infrastructure, for example, taking out signs and decreasing maintenance, also reduce the ease of access, affect visitor numbers in a similar way, and way result in people joining guided tours. Such alterations raise concerns about equity of access to areas that were previously available to a wider range of the community, and are usually done only where there is a strong environmental justification.

Education

Education covers a number of areas, including information dissemination and training and the use of codes of conduct. Educating users in the basic concepts of ecology and minimum impact practices through literature and ranger interaction can be effective, and many people regard this as a vital function of national park management. By advertising the specific attributes of an area, or

Management on Rottnest Island

Rottnest Island, off the south-west coast of Western Australia has about 350,000 annual visitor arrivals, and the number is increasing each year. To maintain the island's environment under this pressure, a combination of management strategies has been adopted. Community consultation was an integral part of the development of these strategies, with residents taking greater control and responsibility for their environment.

An overall strategy involved zoning both the land and marine environments into a settlement area (10 per cent of the island), wildlife reserves (90 per cent), marine reserves, and conservation parks, allowing for different management strategies in each area.

Some areas (such as bird nesting sites) were hardened through the construction of boardwalks which also channel visitors away from sensitive breeding areas. Extensive interpretation services are also provided, educating visitors on a range of environmental practices and technology. Waste management strategies have been introduced, separating solids from waste water and transporting them to the mainland, recycling programs are in place, and energy saving technology is being used.

The combination of community consultation, better practices and visitor "control" have resulted in a sustainable tourism industry on Rottnest Island.

identifying a range of recreational opportunities in surrounding areas, changes in visitor patterns can be achieved.

In areas where exclusion is difficult, education and adherence to codes of conduct may be an important way of reducing management costs. Codes of conduct cover areas such as guidance on places to visit, routes available and preferred conduct, and are examined in Chapter 6.

World Heritage Listing

World Heritage Listing can be applied to any land, not just publicly managed sites. In Australia and New Zealand, World Heritage properties exist on freehold land, pastoral leases, Aboriginal reserves, recreation reserves, town reserves, nature reserves, state forest and national parks. Many people, including tour operators, fear that by listing an area as World Heritage it will be closed off from its current use, or that they will lose control of the land. This is not true.

World Heritage listing does not affect ownership rights, all local laws still apply and management does not pass to any international body. The Commonwealth Government does have an obligation to protect and conserve a World Heritage property but, unless current land use threatens the natural or cultural values of the property, no changes will occur. For example, grazing still occurs at Shark Bay in Western Australia, and recreational and commercial fishing is still undertaken on the Great Barrier Reef, both Word Heritage properties.

World Heritage properties are sites that have exceptional natural and/or cultural values, and the aim of the List is to promote cooperation among nations to protect the natural and cultural heritage of the world. More than 470 sites are listed worldwide, including the Pyramids of Egypt, Westminster Abbey in England, the Great Wall of China and the Grand Canyon in the United States.

In order to qualify for the list, the property must meet a range of specific criteria, such as being an outstanding example of the earth's history or biological processes, or of exceptional natural beauty. Some of the requirements for cultural sites are that they must represent a masterpiece of human creative genius, bear exceptional testimony to a cultural tradition, or be an outstanding example of human design or settlement.

Eleven Australian sites are included on the World Heritage List. If any of them are near you, it would be well worth incorporating them into your ecotourism product. The sites are:

Australia
- The Great Barrier Reef, Queensland
- The Tasmanian Wilderness
- Kakadu National Park, Northern Territory

- Willandra Lakes Region, New South Wales
- The Lord Howe Island Group, New South Wales
- Uluru-Kata Tjuta National Park, Northern Territory
- Central Eastern Rainforest Reserves (Australia), New South Wales and Queensland
- The Wet Tropics of Queensland
- Shark Bay, Western Australia
- Fraser Island, Queensland
- The Australian Fossil Mammal Sites, Riversleigh/Naracoorte, South Australia

New Zealand
- Te Wahipounamu, south-west New Zealand
- Tongariro National Park

The primary management objectives for a World Heritage area include the responsibility to protect, conserve and present the values of each of these areas. The phrase "present the values" indicates that the area must be made available for people to experience. Other objectives are to ensure the property has a function in the life of the community and to use education and information programs to strengthen the appreciation and respect of the area's values. Ecotourism is well placed to play a major role in the presentation, conservation, education and community involvement of World Heritage properties.

Tour Planning and Implementation

Tourism enterprises operating on public land must usually meet a range of criteria set by the land management agencies (National Parks Service, Conservation and Land Management etc.) to gain a permit. All commercial operations on public land in Australia and New Zealand, including logging, mining, bee keeping, and grazing require permits or concessions which usually comprise a fee that is considered appropriate for the commercial use involved.

The permit usually includes a range of practices that a tour operator is permitted (or not) to undertake. These may contain a combination of the land management measures outlined earlier, such as times of year that the activity is permitted, size of groups, track restrictions, designated camp sites, use of campfires and other environmental practices. Most of the requirements are absolutely minimal, and all ecotour operators should exceed them in the normal practice of their business.

Many tour operators also contribute in kind to the maintenance of tracks or campsites. This not only assists the land managers, but also helps to create a better understanding between the two groups, who at times may have felt that their aims conflicted.

Minimising Energy and Water Use in Tour Operations

Energy requirements constitute the single most significant, ongoing environmental impact, and the energy needs of the tour must be met in ways that are as environmentally friendly as possible.

Transport - Land and Water

Transport is a tour operator's main energy outlay — from support vehicles carrying camping and cooking requirements through to people movers — and in many cases has the main environmental impact of a tour. The impacts of transport energy use are not as immediately visible as some other impacts, such as erosion of access tracks, campfire scarring or trampling of plants, so they do not always gain the attention of guests, and operators usually become aware only when they look at their fuel bills. Even when compared with other uses of energy on a tour, fuel for transport is still not as visible as energy used for refrigeration or cooking. Fuel is purchased from petrol stations outside of the national park, with most of the impacts occurring at the production sites, apart from some visible air pollution.

By reducing fuel use, savings will be made, both financially and environmentally. Reductions can be achieved through altering habits and practices on the tour as well as by using fuel-efficient vehicles.

Vehicle use can be reduced by increasing the amount of walking done on a tour and by using non-motorised transport such as mountain bikes or, in certain areas, horses, camels or llamas. Although these animals may not be considered as part of an "ecotour" due to some of the impacts they can have, in some situations they are better suited to the environment than any other form of transport. For example, packhorse tours use no fuel-burning transport, and can utilise campsites that are not accessible by vehicles, thus spreading the use of the land so that other sites can regenerate. In many areas they are a living link with our cultural heritage.

Another way of reducing vehicle use is to plan tours and their support vehicle routes so that they cover the least distance possible, with minimal backtracking. For example, on a hiking tour, guests can hike all day over challenging terrain, but the actual road distance between camps need not be far. As long as they are experiencing what they expect, this will not detract from the tour. It is the journey that is the goal, not the destination.

Driving techniques can also affect fuel consumption. Most vehicles, for example, consume up to 20 per cent less fuel when travelling at 90 km/hour than at 110 km/hour on open roads. By keeping tyre pressures at recommended levels, rolling resistance and fuel consumption is reduced. Pack racks create wind resistance which can increase fuel consumption up to 10 per cent. Many driver training courses demonstrate ways of improving fuel efficiency as well as safety.

Vehicle maintenance also helps to conserve fuel — regular servicing maintains the efficiency of the vehicle. Check with your local service station that the changed oil is being recycled. Most service stations can arrange for oil recycling.

When selecting vehicles for your tour, look for fuel efficiency as well as carrying capacity and other needs. Diesel powered vehicles are 20–40 per cent more fuel efficient than petrol. Four-wheel drive vehicles are used extensively in tour operations, but they may not be necessary. Many tours operate on roads suitable for two-wheel drive vehicles, but operators feel their guests' expectation of adventure requires them to have a four-wheel drive. Often a conventional vehicle with suitable tyres can carry out the tasks just as successfully and with tremendous fuel savings. Educating your clients about the energy efficiency of two-wheel drives and providing "adventure" for them outside the vehicles should solve this dilemma.

If a large vehicle is required only occasionally, consider using a smaller vehicle with a light trailer when the larger capacity is required. This will be more fuel efficient and cost-effective.

When using water transport, the principles are much the same. Fuel efficient water transport includes sailing wherever possible (a great tourist drawcard!), using diesel fuel that is not only more efficient but also has a lower fire risk and four-stroke engines that are more fuel efficient and quieter than the smaller two-stroke ones.

As with other vehicles, fuel consumption on boats increases dramatically at high speeds, and leaving the engine idling wastes fuel. Good inspection and maintenance practices should be carried out so that oil leaks are minimised (preferably eliminated), and keep the hulls clean to minimise drag.

Energy Supplies

Batteries are the most common source of portable energy, and fluorescent lamps powered by rechargeable batteries are the most efficient type of lighting, followed by the mantle-type LPG or kerosene lamps. In the past, tour operators have not used batteries extensively due to the size and number needed on extended tours. Using rechargeable batteries that can be charged by vehicle alternators or renewable energy sources, reduces the number required.

Photovoltaic cells (as described in the next chapter) can provide solar power for refrigeration as well as lighting, and water can be heated for bush showers by direct sunlight.

Portable diesel generators are another energy source, but many of them are noisy and can detract from the atmosphere of the tour. They are not as efficient as rechargeable batteries or solar power, and are banned in some parks and reserves.

If wood is used for energy, it is important not to take it from protected areas. Many logs provide homes for wildlife and are an important part of the ecosystem. Determine what is acceptable and use an ecologically sustainable source, such as a wood lot.

Refrigeration

Save energy by reducing refrigeration requirements, for example, by using non-perishable foods such as dried, tinned, vacuum-sealed or UHT treated food. Frozen food and drinks stay cold for days in a well insulated container, and obtaining supplies on tour will also help to minimise the amount of refrigeration required.

Good insulation is essential in all forms of refrigeration, and doubling the thickness of the insulation in a refrigerator can halve the energy consumption. If you are using insulated ice boxes, by transferring the day's food and drink requirements from the main one to smaller eskies, the main ice box need only be opened once a day, preferably in the cool of the morning. This will save a great deal of ice-melt.

If you require a refrigerator or freezer, choose one that is appropriate to your needs and is energy-efficient. Portable refrigerators range from a capacity of 35

Energy-efficient Refrigeration

The major problem for Albury based tour operator, Champagne Sunset Tours in conducting remote area tours was keeping perishables cold. After many flat batteries from an inefficient portable refrigerator, food floating in melted ice water, and difficulties in keeping up the required supply of ice in remote areas, the company decided to make some changes. In many areas they could not use a portable generator, to comply with national park regulations.

The company developed a system that generates enough power to cover their refrigeration, cooking and heating water requirements in remote areas. The vehicle and trailer are fitted with solar modules that can supply all 12 volt accessories while the vehicle is stationary, including their communication network.

By selecting a 30 litre refrigerator/freezer with the lowest power consumption available and self diagnostic testing, the unit operates at optimum, producing a remarkably low power draw. The trailer operates as a stand-alone unit with a solar module and deep cycle battery, feeding a range of DC and AC equipment including an 80 litre refrigerator/freezer. The operator pre-chills the refrigerators and their contents from mains electricity before leaving.

litres to 150 litres and can run off various power levels, from 12 volt to 24 volt DC, 240 volt AC or LPG. The 12 and 24 volt models can be run off car batteries or photovoltaic (solar) panels, whereas the 240 volt models require a generator or batteries with an inverter. Where power is not available, LPG is effective.

Cooking

Open fires have been used extensively as a means for cooking in the bush. Tourists appreciate their ambience and the taste of the food which is different from what they normally eat — important aspects of the tourism experience.

A cooking fire should be small, and use the minimum amount of wood — not a great bonfire. However, it is not always possible or practical to use wood. Many tour operators are required to cart their own wood, which is bulky and heavy, adding to the load of the vehicles.

Fires can also scar the environment, so should be lit in the same place every time and kept under one square metre in size to minimise this effect. Apart from the visual aspect of a fire scar, nothing will grow where they have been. By minimising their spread you are maximising nature.

If a renewable source of firewood is not readily available, LPG fuel stoves are preferable as they do not contaminate or scar sensitive environments.

Fire restrictions may decide for you what type of cooking will be done — fuel stoves or open fires cannot be used on days of total fire ban. It is your responsibility to find out when there is a fire ban, so if in doubt don't light up. On total fire ban days appliances in a caravan or caravan-type trailer (but not in a tent, annexe or tent-like trailer) may be used provided they are attended at all times. Some parks provide built-in electric or gas barbeques, which can be used as long as they are within ten metres of a water supply and are surrounded by a three-metre area clear of all flammable material.

When planning a tour, take the probability of a fire ban into account and provide alternative food that does not require cooking. Be aware of local fire restrictions that may not allow the lighting of fires in certain sensitive areas ("fuel stove only" areas), and avoid lighting fires on dry, windy days regardless of whether there are official restrictions.

Make sure the fire is out before leaving the campsite, and use water not soil to dampen it, as fires can maintain their heat even when smothered with soil. If the ground underneath the coals is still warm, the fire is not out. Do not use fires in areas that have peat soils, such as much of western Tasmania, as they can burn underground for weeks.

Washing

Disposable plates and cutlery are an absolute "no" for any environmentally conscious tour operator. Reusable dishes are preferable, no matter how well the waste is managed, as the first imperative of waste management is to reduce the amount.

As a way of saving time and water, dishes can be scraped clean and stored in a bag until the end of the day when all the washing up is done at once.

As for clothes washing, manually operated portable washing machines that require only one bucket of water are readily available.

Re-use cuts costs

Odyssey Safaris, in the Northern Territory no longer uses noisy generators on tour. The company uses portable, 60 litre 12 volt refrigerators powered by vehicle alternators while on the move, and spare batteries powered by a solar photovoltaic panel when stationary.

To minimise washing up, guests are assigned a colour-coded cup which staff wash at the end of each day. As the cups are being re-used throughout the day, fewer are needed which in turn saves on storage space and cost. Odyssey estimates that the total cost (including washing) of a re-useable cup is $23 per year, compared with a cost of $54 for the number of disposable cups that would be used per customer over one year.

Sewage and Waste Disposal on Tour

The handling of human faecal waste should be a major concern of any tour operator who is using an area without toilet facilities. Where possible, operators should utilise the systems that have been built by local councils or public land management agencies, but in many remote and semi-remote areas such systems do not exist.

Free Disposal

Free disposal may be necessary in areas where there are no toilet facilities, but it is only viable in places that are under-used as nutrients released can affect ecosystems and health. Faecal waste must be handled responsibly to avoid gastroenteritis and giardia. Giardia is a human bacterial parasite which can cause chronic diarrhoea. It has been found in some alpine areas of Australia and New Zealand in mountain streams that have been contaminated by faecal waste, and must not spread to other areas.

To avoid the spread of giardia and to limit occurrences of gastroenteritis, all human waste must be disposed at least 100 metres from any water source, and buried at least 15 cm deep. Toilet paper should be buried with the waste, and all should be mixed with soil to help decomposition and to discourage animals. Sanitary pads, tampons and condoms should be sealed in plastic bags and carried out.

In the snow it is important that the hole is dug into the soil, not just the snow as the waste will become exposed when the snow melts. If you are operating in high-use areas, snow or narrow river valleys, it is worth considering carrying human wastes out to a sewage system. However, this will need to be carefully considered and dealt with in relation to the attitudes of your guests — even western cultural taboos can be extremely strong in relation to the handling of human waste. Many city dwellers find burying their waste adventurous enough!

Chemical Toilets

Some tour operators use chemical toilets containing a chemical concoction that treats wastes. The strength of the chemicals requires them to be emptied into a mains sewer, not into the environment either directly or via septic seepage. One chemical toilet, known as the "honey-loo", uses a sugary substance that seems to be more environmentally sound than the normal chemicals.

Sewage on Boats

Avoid dumping sewage off boats. Many harbours provide pump-out facilities, but if they don't, request that they do. Local councils and water boards may be able to help in this area.

Waste Water

Any water that contains detergents and soaps must be handled responsibly. Do not wash within 50 metres of a water course, as even biodegradable soap and toothpaste can harm fish and water life. Scatter wash water so that it filters through the soil before returning to the water source, and do not throw food scraps into streams or lakes.

If possible, keep all clothes washing until after the tour. In this way, the environment will be saved from coping with soapy waste water.

Rubbish

Rubbish should not be burnt or buried as animals are likely to dig it up and scatter it. Also, disturbing the soil by repeated digging can encourage weeds and erosion. Leaving scraps in the bush, particularly at a regular camp or picnic site, encourages unnaturally high, unbalanced animal populations that become dependent on these scraps. Although the animals may be cute, they can become a nuisance and develop diseases from eating refined foods.

If you come across rubbish left by others, you will not only help the environment by taking their rubbish out, but also provide your guests with an example of good environmental practice. Many tour operators put considerable effort into keeping the sites they use clean of all rubbish, regardless of whose it is, as it affects the enjoyment of their guests. Litter is one of the issues most commented on by nature-based tourists as it is highly visible and unattractive.

Minimising Environmental Impacts on Tour

Many activities form part of an ecotour (eg fishing or bird watching), or make up the whole tour (eg camping or bush walking). All of these activities have some impact on the environment, and many of the public land management agencies have developed codes of practice, recommendations and regulations as to how they are carried out. As well as minimising energy use and waste as described above, an ecotourism operator should be responsible about setting up camps, using tracks and trails and other procedures.

While regulations will vary from state to state, the behaviour outlined below should be adopted as the minimum requirement for responsible environmental behaviour.

Camping

Camping is a popular way of enjoying the outdoors, and many tour operators, from large bus companies down to small, personalised tours, incorporate some camping into their trips. Tours that focus on walking, horse riding, canoeing or any other form of transport apart from vehicles may carry their equipment with them or in support vehicles that they meet at the end of the day's activities. Either way, the minimum impact practices are the same.

The use of fires, and disposal of sewage and wastes as discussed above, apply to all camping activities.

When setting up a camp site, consider its aspect and camp at least 30 metres from rivers and other water courses. Any prevailing winds or weather patterns will indicate where to place shelters or windbreaks as well as keeping the campfire from catching any litter or smoking out the kitchen tent/area. Remember, wherever possible light the campfire (if you are using one) on a site that has been used previously.

Boggy or vegetated areas will suffer damage extremely quickly, so look for low impact campsites with sandy or hard surfaces. Spending no more than two nights at any one site will allow the area to recover.

Modern waterproof tents with floors and tent poles are easy to use and have less impact on the environment than heavy, dark canvas tents. Trenches around the tents won't be needed if you plan where to pitch them and use well-drained sites.

Snow Camping

Snow protects alpine vegetation and soils from many of the impacts associated with camping but a few guidelines should be followed. People camp in igloos, snow caves or snowproof tents, and the camp site can be almost anywhere as there should be no long-lasting signs of the camp. The most significant impact of snow camping is the disposal of waste, discussed above — make sure that it is either buried in the soil or carried out with you. The sight of used toilet paper floating around on the spring breezes is not attractive.

As with any site, ensure it is well protected from prevailing winds and possible storms, and beware that some slopes may be prone to avalanches. If you decide to stay in a hut, remember that most huts in the Australian Alps are only for emergency or refuge use, and can be used by everyone, so it is important not to take one over for the exclusive use of your tour group. (Holders of grazing leases have a prior right to use of the huts in most circumstances). On leaving the hut, make sure it is clean, replace any firewood you have used, and make sure that any fires are out — huts can still burn down in winter. Many huts in New Zealand can be reserved, but they are extremely popular, so early reservation and arrival at the hut is often required. It is important to consider carrying camping equipment and not to rely on huts even when booked, as the more popular ones can be crowded, noisy and uncomfortable.

Bushwalking

With the growing interest in bushwalking, many popular walking areas are becoming severely affected by the numbers of people using them. If there are tracks, encourage your guests to stay on them even if they are rough and muddy. Cutting corners on steep zig-zag tracks and walking on their edges will increase the damage and visual scarring and contribute to erosion. Where there are no tracks in open country, spreading out will disperse the impact. Each time you visit a trackless area choose a different route and, if possible, camp at different sites.

As an ecotour operator, you should know what types of vegetation are sensitive to trampling and be able to encourage guests to stay on hard ground wherever possible. Heavy walking boots can damage sensitive terrain, so recommend footwear that is appropriate for your area — solid, lightweight walking boots are good in most Australian and New Zealand conditions (apart from the more rugged areas in the South), and sandshoes can be worn on many tracks. Soft footwear such as sandshoes should be encouraged around campsites.

Spotlighting

Spotlighting is an excellent way for people to experience wildlife, much of which is nocturnal. However, many animals are extremely sensitive to light and spotlights may affect their eyesight. Keep the number of lights to the minimum you need to ensure group safety — issuing every member with a light will create confusion and may distress many animals.

When looking for eyes shining in the dark, low wattage lights or small torches with a maximum of 60 watts should be sufficient, then for observing the animals even lower wattages should be used, down to 30 watts. Placing a red filter in front of the spotlight once the animal has been located will reduce the intensity of that light while you are observing them. Although they are more expensive, infra-red binoculars are an excellent piece of equipment for observing nightlife as they do not use any damaging rays.

Keeping noise levels down is also important, so try to brief guests before setting out. When you wish to address the group, wait until they are all within easy listening range. A second guide at the rear who can provide information and answer questions, will stop people crowding to the front of the group, and the leader having to shout. The "tail" guide will also provide additional safety.

As many nocturnal animals tend to live in trees, your guests are likely to be walking along in the dark looking up, not at the track. Using clearly defined, well maintained tracks so they do not have to concentrate on where they are putting their feet will increase their enjoyment and reduce accidents.

If you wish to spotlight on public land, by offering to provide the local land managers with details of nightly counts of sightings, you may be permitted to use areas that are locked at night, such as established picnic grounds that also have well-maintained paths and tracks.

Rock Climbing and Abseiling

Rock climbing and abseiling are growing in popularity as outdoor adventure activities, and some sites in Australia, such as Mt Arapiles in Victoria, are world class. Many of these sites are away from standard tourist routes, but have experienced a surge in visitor numbers that has severely affected the surrounding camping areas as well as the actual rock-faces. Minimum impact camping techniques must be followed.

Rock climbers and abseilers should avoid areas where birds nest, and refrain from wire brushing to remove mosses in cracks and gullies. Excess use of fixed equipment and chalk, chipping of rock and the use of bolts must be carefully considered, as all these activities, while not significant by themselves, can build up to create major long-term environmental impacts.

Trail Bikes and Four-Wheel Drives

Generally speaking, all trail bikes and four-wheel drive vehicles must remain on formed roads, and trail bikes are banned from walking tracks. Off-road driving is generally prohibited. Most beaches, dunes and coastal reserves are off limits to four-wheel drives and trail bikes, apart from a few such as Fraser

Island in Queensland, Peron Dunes and Sandy Cape in Tasmania. If you are driving on such a beach, enter at the designated points and try to avoid vegetated dunes, as vehicles can easily remove the fragile cover, leading to extreme erosion. Always drive below the high tide mark, as above this mark, not only is the sand less compacted, but birds lay their eggs in small scrapes on the soft sand. Chicks tend to hide in the seaweed and are difficult to see, so keep to the harder wet sand, especially in breeding season.

If you come across a puddle in the middle of a dirt road, try not to widen the track or make a new one by going around it into the bush, as this will only increase the damage. Sometimes it may be inevitable, so look for the best way to handle the situation. By being aware of road conditions you may be able to avoid problems by taking alternate routes. If there is a fallen tree or branch blocking the way, remove it rather than going around it and widening the track.

When crossing streams and rivers, use the existing entry and exit points if bridges or culverts are not provided, and if you need to winch a vehicle, wherever possible winch from another vehicle rather than around trees, which can be easily damaged. If you have to use a tree, use protective padding or webbing. Wheel chains should only be used as a last resort as they can be extremely damaging to tracks, creating even more problems for those who follow.

Because of the noise pollution accompanying trail bikes (and some four-wheel drive vehicles), many tourists may not consider them environmentally "acceptable". You will need to consider your market carefully if you are planning to include trail bikes in your ecotours.

Mountain Bikes

Over the past few years, mountain bike riding has taken off. It is seen by many as an environmentally sound alternative to motorised transport. In the past, some mountain bike users have tended to "fly" down tracks, out of control, endangering themselves and others. Proper guiding and instruction should be able to overcome this on your tours. Skidding can damage tracks and lead to erosion, but by keeping to the middle of the tracks, little damage will be done. As with walking (and driving), muddy tracks should be avoided wherever possible, as tyre tracks will channel water into new areas, and increase erosion.

Bicycles are allowed on most roads and tracks that permit four-wheel drive vehicles, as well as some designated tracks, but they should be kept off narrow bushwalking tracks.

Many of the tracks used by mountain bikes may be shared with horse riders. Bike riders must give horses the right of way, and be aware that a frightened horse can be dangerous. Dismount, announce your presence and keep talking as the horse and riders pass — this reassures the animal. By being alert for signs of horses, such as hoof prints, on the track, you will be prepared for them.

Horse and Camel Riding

Although horse riding is not always regarded as an appropriate ecotourism activity, in some cases it may be less harmful than motorised transport. Operators may offer horse riding as an adventure activity outside the "eco" aspect of their tour, so it is important that they understand how to manage horses in the bush. Camels are included under this heading because they have similar impacts (apart from having soft feet) so many of the same rules apply.

Regulations governing where horses can be ridden vary in each state and territory of Australia and New Zealand. In some cases they are permitted in certain areas of national parks, while others only allow them on formed roads. However, a number of basic principles apply at all times. Horses can transport weeds into an area through their manure, so they should only be fed weed-free processed feed or clean chaff and cracked grain that will not germinate. This feed should be commenced 24 to 48 hours before the start of the tour, so that the animal's system is "clean". Using nosebags prevents spillage, and also ensures that each horse is getting enough feed.

Keep to designated tracks, don't cut corners on zig-zag tracks, and spread out in open country where there are no trails.

Camping with horses increases trampling and grazing impacts, so use designated horse camps with yards, or a low power, battery operated electric fence. Yards should be as large as possible to reduce the impacts of grazing and trampling. Don't tether horses to trees as they may damage them and trample and compact the soil. Break up and scatter manure before leaving the campsite, as this is a major visual impact at campsites and on trails. Horses should be held at least 30 metres from all water courses, watered downstream from any campsites and must be washed, away from streams.

Rafting and Canoeing

As a tour operator, you will most likely need to transport a number of canoes or rafts to a launching area. Leave the transport vehicles on formed roads and tracks and carry the craft to the water.

When selecting camp sites on the river, be sure they have a robust bank or beach that will withstand landing and launching, and find sites that are big enough to enable you to camp 30 metres from the watercourse.

Waste and rubbish may need to be carried out from particularly sensitive areas.

Boating and Sailing

The importance of disposing of waste and sewage back in dock has already been discussed, but other rubbish can cause severe environmental problems. A classic example is the plastic rings from six-pack cans of drink which do not degrade and can kill mammals, birds and fish that get caught in them. Dispose of all rubbish on land.

Fishing

Lost fishing line is another common hazard for wildlife. It is often lost through being poorly tied or worn or is just thrown away. Check equipment regularly and increase its lifespan by storing it in a dark place. Always thoroughly clean the equipment after use, particularly if you are going into different areas, as lines and rods can carry disease.

Dispose of fish remains carefully, as they can attract European wasps if left in rubbish bins. The best option is to take the remains with you and compost them. Throwing remains into lakes and streams is not an alternative as few aquatic animals are large enough to eat them.

Collection of live bait may be permitted in some areas, but even native worms are a part of the food chain, so alternatives such as processed bait, commercial worms or lures should be used. Some anglers have taken to using rod rests made from willow, which is not native to Australia or New Zealand and quickly takes root if left in the ground. You will see evidence throughout the country of willow trees clogging up waterways — do not contribute to this problem.

Fishing regulations vary between states and territories so find out the permissible fishing methods, legal lengths and bag limits for your area. As a tour operator you may be able to get an overall fishing permit for your guests, otherwise they will all have to be issued with them according to state/territory regulations.

Whale Watching and Dolphin Swimming

An activity that is increasing in popularity, and is included in many ecotours, is whale watching and swimming with dolphins. The large number of vessels sometimes observed close to whale and dolphin pods is causing concern and has prompted calls for regulation.

Guidelines that should be adopted by tour operators include not positioning vessels in the path of a pod and refraining from actively chasing pods. Vessels should take particular care of a pod that has a mother and calf in it, especially if they are within 300 metres. No more than three vessels should be within 300 metres of any pod at the one time. Radio communication with other vessels will help to maintain safety of the pod and equity of access to all.

Swimming with whales or dolphins may be permitted in some areas, but authorisation must be given by the responsible statutory body. If swimming with the mammals, don't chased them, rather give them the opportunity to come to you.

You may need to remind your guests that whales and dolphins are wild animals and should be given the respect due to all wild creatures.

Encounters with Dolphins

New Zealand dolphin tours enterprise, Dolphin Encounters, has a concession from the Department of Conservation to operate its tours. The number of swimmers in the water is limited to small groups of between 10 and 13 on two boats only, which minimises the impact of vessels visiting the dolphins and swimmers interacting with them.

Guests are given an on-board commentary covering information about the dolphins and the environmental impacts of pollution and improper fishing practices as well as some local history background.

At the end of the tour, each guest is given a personalised information pack which includes:

- A Dusky Dolphin information sheet
- A conservation sheet, listing contact addresses of conservation groups around the world, enabling visitors to make contact with a local group when they get home
- A postcard of the dolphins
- A tour brochure

Snorkelling, Scuba Diving and Coral Viewing

All divers must avoid contact with flora, fauna and substrata, so standing on, or grasping, corals or kelp must be discouraged, and all dragging equipment such as gauges and hoses must be secured. As it is not possible to talk underwater, a "guided tour" may require some items to be picked up and brought to the surface so that they can be explained. All items that are picked up (living or dead) must be returned to their exact position.

Don't chase or handle free swimming animals or block their paths. Once again, they are wild animals and must be permitted to interact on their own terms, if at all.

Collecting any items for souvenirs (or any other purpose) is actively discouraged, unless local exemptions apply, such as for an indigenous or scientific group.

Feeding and Handling Wild Animals

Wild animals have been mentioned a few times in the points above, and all ecotourism operators should adopt some general criteria. As already pointed out, feeding wild animals (including marine life) can create an imbalanced ecosystem, with the animals reliant on handouts. Scraps of processed food can cause diseases like lumpy jaw in kangaroos, but even feeding food that the animals normally consume can create problems of unbalanced populations.

Many tour operators feed animals to ensure their guests will see some wildlife, but this practice cannot be condoned as a part of ecotourism. If your guests have been prepared well enough, they will appreciate chance encounters far more than the contrived, "force feeding" episodes.

Handling wild animals is also an important issue. While promotion of Australia overseas still relies heavily on images of tourists cuddling koalas, such handling stresses the animals and is not permitted in all states/territories. This difference between visitor expectations and reality, creates problems, which can be overcome through effective education and interpretation.

If wild animals are being handled, they must have an "escape route" so that that they can move away if they become stressed.

Spreading of Weeds and Plant Diseases
Weeds and plant diseases such as the widespread cinnamon fungus (*Phytophthora cinnamonmi*) are spread into new areas by moving infected plant material or soil on muddy boots, trowels, tent pegs, in car tyre treads, horse hooves etc. What is a native plant endemic to one area may become a weed in another so make sure equipment and boots are kept clean and washed where they are used.

Bush Etiquette
Many of the areas you visit will have other people there as well —very few areas that are attractive to people are completely solitary. So, it is important that all groups can enjoy themselves.

Often individual or small groups of walkers and campers hoping for solitude and peace feel threatened by the noise and size of tour groups. Even small tour groups can be relatively noisy, as many people take an ecotour for social as well as environmental reasons. You need to respect other people's need for solitude, while still keeping your group happy. Usually, just by being friendly, telling them what you are doing and how long you intend to be there will overcome any problems.

If you are on a trail bike or mountain bike and see horse riders, make sure the horses can hear you — if you turn off your engine and coast pass them they will most likely get a fright and possibly injure themselves, their riders or your guests. Talking as you go past is often the best option. Walkers can also be frightened by silent mountain bikes!

Of course, if you are riding the horse, a friendly attitude and awareness that the physical size of a horse is intimidating to anyone on the ground will help reduce any ill-feeling towards you. Fear and misunderstanding can often be the underlying cause of negative attitudes towards horses.

It is considered common courtesy in the bush to stop and say hello to anyone you may pass on a track or trail, and this friendliness is something that your guests will also appreciate and enjoy. You will also get invaluable information on the condition of tracks, campsites and other groups that may be around.

Partnerships in Managing Tour Impacts

As an individual tour operator you may be concerned about maintaining the environmental integrity of the areas you visit but unsure how to do it when so many other groups and individuals use the same places. Forming partnerships with the public land managers and other users through a "user's group" or association and developing codes of practice and other programs can benefit everyone, and the environment. Increased understanding of the needs of each group, and cooperation between groups are positive outcomes which all stakeholders should aim for.

Industry & Government Work Together

The Cod Hole is a popular diving site on the Great Barrier Reef. Tourism operators require a permit to operate in the area but in the past their behaviour was not restricted. The increased "people pressure", combined with some natural changes (such as a crown-of-thorns starfish infestation) resulted in a number of changes to the area, including an increased population of small predatory fish and competition by moray eels for food handouts.

In 1992 the regular tour operators and management staff of the Great Barrier Reef Marine Park Authority (GBRMPA) formed an association to develop management objectives and a code of practice for the Cod Hole area. The code relates to areas such as mooring use and anchoring, diver behaviour, fish feeding, interpretation, and scheduling of visits. As the code was developed by the industry as a form of self-regulation, and not imposed "from above", the operators have adopted it enthusiastically.

The benefits to the tourism industry are long-term sustainability of a popular destination, improved safety and visitor experience, and an enhanced environmental reputation. The tourism industry has also gained a better understanding of GBRMPA's management objectives and the issues it has to deal with.

Trail Riders Help to Minimise Impact

Yarra Brae Trail Rides in Kinglake, Victoria felt that its future was in jeopardy due to limitations being imposed by the National Parks Service. The Department of Conservation and Natural Resources, on the other hand, was concerned about the impact of horses on wet trails and tracks in the national park surrounding the property.

Meetings were held to identify the problems of each group, and the Department agreed that if Yarra Brae provided practical assistance with track maintenance, the horses' impact would be limited to certain areas which could be minimised and controlled.

As well as providing much of the material required, Yarra Brae staff worked with Departmental staff on the tracks. This created a practical level of understanding between those actually working in the field, so that future issues could be dealt with quickly before they escalated.

This cooperation resolved Yarra Brae's financial concerns as well as the social and environmental issues of the National Parks Service.

Land Care

Land degradation, particularly erosion and salinity, affects over half of Australia and New Zealand's rural land. The current generation of farmers is paying for the self-centred actions of the past, and many recognise that this exploitation could continue until the land actually dies. In 1989, the Land Care program was introduced to Australia with a federal umbrella body, Land Care Australia Limited, to oversee the program on a national level, supported by state Land Care Committees. The Landcare Trust was introduced in New Zealand in 1996 (even though there have been associated groups for over 40 years) and is based loosely on the successful Australian model.

Land Care is part of the broader framework of environmental conservation, focussing on sustainable production from the land (covering crops and domestic animal production, water quality and supply) as well as the broader components of wildlife, scientific values, aesthetics and recreation.

The support base of Land Care are the Land Care committees — local community groups comprising land-owners involved in farming, mining, forestry, public lands and local government. The actual make-up of each committee differs depending on the region and the particular needs of the community. Many committees are run by enthusiastic land-owners who believe strongly in an industry-driven Land Care organisation, while others are driven more by local government. The nature of the driving force often depends on the commitment and enthusiasm of individuals. Two years after the introduction of Land Care, more than 1000 local Land Care Committees (LCC) existed in Australia. Your nearest group can be found through your local council.

Local conservation groups also contribute to some of the schemes planned and implemented by district Land Care committees. As ecotourism operators have a commitment to local conservation, by incorporating these projects into tours or donating a percentage of the takings to Land Care schemes, you will also be providing support for the local community.

Principles of Land Care

Land Care subscribes to four basic principles:

1. Prevention is better than cure.
2. Rehabilitation may not always be the best response to land degradation as it may be too costly in relation to the returns, and alternatives must be considered. Severely degraded land may be put to other uses, such as providing areas for buildings that would otherwise be built on non-degraded land. For example, farm buildings and yards or tourist accommodation could be built in those areas.
3. Land degradation problems are as much social as technical. Education through ecotourism offers other ways of dealing with these issues, such as correcting human behaviour and the habits of generations. Providing farmers with a tangible, immediate financial boost where people pay to assist with rehabilitation programs will also assist in shifting community attitudes towards sustainable practices.
4. Vegetative cover is the key to land protection. This sounds simple, but considering the extent of totally cleared land in this country, it is a message that is taking a long time to be heard.

While many landowners accept that Land Care and rehabilitation are important for the future of the land, many still feel they cannot afford to forego commercial production on part of their land "merely" to conserve biodiversity. One response to this position has been landholders seeking compensation for the protection of flora and fauna on their properties. Most governments seem unwilling to commit the sums required to provide fair compensation, but instead want to educate landowners to consider the long-term economic benefits of maintaining productive land as its own reward. However, this does not solve the immediate issue of funding Land Care programs. Tourism has the potential to assist in this crucial area by giving "non-productive" land a value and capacity to earn income which may assist in off-setting rehabilitation costs.

Ecotourism and Land Care

One of the major concerns identified at the first Land Care forum held in 1990 was the lack of urban support and the limited resources of people, time and money. Extensive media coverage has made the general public more aware of the socio-economic significance of land degradation and increasingly city people want to find out for themselves what is happening on the land, and what can be done.

Ecotourism offers an opportunity to educate these people in Land Care and land management. Many ecotourists will take this improved understanding home with them and discuss what they have learnt with others, creating the opportunity for support from people in cities and towns who may otherwise have no real perception of what is happening in the environment. This support has the potential to provide flow-on economic benefits by bringing more ecotourists to the area as well as providing political and financial support from the city.

Some groups of ecotourists are also interested in active participation while on holiday, such as helping with reafforestation and undertaking data gathering for research activities. They may be students, farmers, belong to a conservation group or just interested individuals. The interest and enthusiasm of these people to assist in land rehabilitation programs can be harnessed through ecotourism and the Land Care program.

Some of the groups interested in active participation are: the Australian Trust for Conservation Volunteers (involved in tree planting, seed collecting and track maintenance), Earthwatch — an international non-profit organisation that places volunteers to work with scientists in the field, and the Australian and New Zealand Scientific Exploration Society, which conducts scientific expeditions into wilderness areas. Appendix Three contains contact details for these groups.

Degraded Sites as a Tourist Attraction

Land that has been severely degraded beyond foreseeable redemption can be used as demonstration areas to show the damage people can cause. For example, tourists visiting Tasmania are fascinated by the bare hills next to the Queenstown smelter. This site is severely degraded and is a marked contrast to the image that Tasmania presents as a land of natural, untouched wonders. This contrast makes the impact of the site even more powerful, and with good interpretation, visitors take home an understanding of how such a situation can occur.

Property-owners may not be proud to display degraded sites on their land, but they can be a source of income, education and provide the basis for rehabilitation.

Conclusion

Many of the environmentally sound activities undertaken by tour operators will not be automatically noticed by most of their guests. Often the high-profile examples of recycling are not possible, practical or the most environmentally efficient means available, regardless of tourist perceptions. Therefore, it is important for tourism operators to promote their minimum impact policies and explain the procedures. By explaining to tourists why their human wastes should be buried 100 metres from a river they will be more willing to cooperate, and also appreciate your knowledge of the range of issues that affect the environment.

By working with environmental initiatives such as Land Care, ecotourism can provide tangible benefits to local communities and educate people in an easy, non-threatening manner through practical, working demonstrations.

5 Working with the Environment

Ecotourism relies heavily on the environment — without it, there would be no tourism. All tourism operators, not just ecotourism ventures, should adopt the procedures covered in this chapter. However, with their commitment to enhancing and protecting the environment, ecotourism operations must be especially conscious and aware of all aspects of working with the environment through sound environmental practices such as energy conservation and waste minimisation. The impact of structures, roads, waste discharges and other tourist services and facilities must not harm the local ecosystem or affect the historical integrity or visual attraction of the area, otherwise the very aspects that bring tourists to the region may be lost.

Improving an operation's environmental performance need not increase costs or reduce comfort and convenience. On the contrary, many of the alternatives now offered actually save money (eg some of the renewable energy sources and passive building designs). For example, by not changing towels or bed linen every day, cleaning costs and the potential environmental impact of the cleaning materials are reduced, and the life of the items extended.

Even when simple solutions are not available and more costly treatment methods may need to be considered, many intangible benefits, such as enhancing the tourism product in the eyes of the tourists, are possible. The responsible actions of tourism operators, such as energy and waste minimisation, are positive marketable commodities that can be included in promotional material and used as a basis for media articles and promotions.

Building Design, Construction and Operation

Considering the growing interest in the environment and its sustainable use, the lack of "green" (environmentally sound) accommodation is surprising. Of course, the cost and long-term nature of building mean that change tends to be adopted slowly. The predominance of motels no longer meeting the needs of many travellers in rural areas reflects that slowness, as well as a lack of understanding of the changing nature of travellers. Many of today's travellers (business people as well as tourists) are looking for a more personalised attitude towards their accommodation, and also want country accommodation to relate closely to its environment, both cultural and natural. They seek a quality experience, and people choosing ecotourism experiences especially expect tourism operators to perform to high environmental standards.

Environmental construction not only relates to accommodation, but also to information centres, attractions, cafes and restaurants, public infrastructure and other buildings. Even theme parks (large and small) should be able to operate sustainably.

If your area is high in ecotourism assets and attractions, other ecotourism operators as well as independent ecotourists will tend to favour green accommodation, and it could be the deciding factor to visit an area.

Characteristics of Green Accommodation

Green accommodation should tend to reflect the character of the region by utilising historic buildings or precincts, focussing on farmstays in rural farming districts, wilderness lodges near national parks, seaside cottages in fishing villages, and so on.

Most ecotourism accommodation is small scale and locally owned, however some larger-scale developments have adopted a sustainable attitude and are also working to rehabilitate their site or the surrounding land. Some

Green Planning

A proposed resort lodge for Tairua, Coromandel, New Zealand, was required to incorporate a number of environmental considerations into its proposal before meeting approval from the various consent authorities. The proposal involved siting the lodge buildings appropriately for the topography of the area, and leaving natural valleys, watercourses and areas of good vegetation intact. A vegetation rehabilitation program aimed at replacing the existing exotic forest with native forest was proposed, and any vegetation removal was to be replanted immediately to minimise any adverse effects.

Stormwater was to be piped from all hard surfaces such as road, parking areas and buildings to be discharged over a natural waterfall at the boundary of the site, and pedestrian footbridges over watercourses were designed to have minimal impact.

The proposal was given approval, and illustrates the benefits of taking environmental considerations on board at the initial proposal/planning stages.

examples of larger accommodation include Kingfisher Bay Resort and Couran Cove Resort, two of the case studies examined in this chapter. Smaller scale examples are Gipsy Point Lodge and Arkaroola.

A high guest-host interaction enables green accommodation providers to encourage their guests to engage in sustainable activities through the range that they offer, the tour operators they recommend, or merely by example.

Due to the dispersed nature of areas of interest to ecotourists, accommodation need not be clustered around major attractions. Spreading the accommodation also spreads the benefits and minimises the impacts. Employment opportunities for the local community are a central part of green accommodation, particularly in the ecotourism context, as well as providing other economic opportunities for the local community such as purchasing local goods and services.

Building Regulations and Environmental Impact Assessment

Building permits are issued by local councils, who may have specific regulations relating not only to zoning (industrial, commercial, residential) but also to the style of building permitted. For example, buildings in the main street of Sorrento, a Victorian seaside town, must be faced with limestone in order to maintain the visual, historical ambience of the streetscape — a great tourism asset. Consultation with local councils and planning bodies will provide information on building regulations, surrounding patterns of development, access and the provision of services that will enable you to develop a proposal that is compatible and likely to be approved.

Many tourism developments, particularly the larger resorts, will be required by either council, state/territory, or federal government legislation to undertake an Environmental Impact Assessment (EIA) of their proposal before any planning approval is given. Not all proposals require an EIA, depending on the state or territory legislation, but operators who subscribe to the ecotourism ethic (or even consider using the term as a marketing tool) should undertake some form of impact assessment. This also provides the operator with information to "fall back on" if there is an environmental backlash or concern regarding the development.

General Criteria to be Considered in an EIA

The level of detail in an EIA will depend on the location, size and nature of the proposal, however it is important that any developer, regardless of the size of the development, avoids interfering with the heritage, cultural or environmental importance of the site in any way that may reduce its intrinsic value. Infrastructure such as buildings and facilities should be provided without causing unnecessary environmental damage. This will usually be most easily (and economically) achieved by utilising naturally hardened, or already impacted and degraded areas.

Access for vehicles, pedestrians or boats may need to be improved in relation to the estimated increase in the number and type of traffic to and from the development during both the construction phase and when it is operational. One way to minimise the cost and extent of additional access routes is to locate the development as close to existing transport routes as possible.

Minimising vegetation clearance is important, but flooding and bushfire danger must also be considered, with options covered to minimise their possibility and manage them if they occur.

Allow scope for future expansion when developing the EIA — many tourism operators have found that lack of expansion has not only affected their own growth but also had an impact on the sale value of the business. Gaining approval for future development at an early stage can be much easier as the councillors involved in granting approval will have a detailed understanding of the overall development strategy and the environmental issues. Applying for approval at a later stage may involve new councillors who have to be informed about the background of the whole development. This can be extremely time-consuming.

Official requirements for an Environmental Impact Assessment vary from state to state, but the process is similar, and includes a report to the relevant minister (usually an Environmental Impact Statement) and release of this statement for public review and comment. The administering authority then evaluates the public comment to help the government make its decision.

The three key elements of an Environmental Impact Assessment are: scoping, alternatives and strategies.

Scoping

The first stage is deciding on the scope of the study by identifying the most likely impacts of the development and determining the level of detail of the assessment. Impacts may include for example, erosion caused by increased water run-off from sealed access roads and compaction of soils around the site, deterioration of the water system through leaching of wastes into rivers, and destruction or degradation of the habitat of endangered plant and animal species through construction or anticipated visitor activity and recreational facilities.

By recognising the potential impacts, you will be able to identify areas of land that are most suitable for building and retain important features such as vegetation and physical characteristics. Significant views that should be maintained or enhanced, and climatic influences should also be included in the scope of the assessment.

Kingfisher Bay Resort

Planning and construction of the Kingfisher Bay Resort on Fraser Island, Queensland, began a few years before the area was included on the World Heritage List. The developers had already recognised the intrinsic beauty and value of the area and were intent on building a state-of-the-art ecotourism property. The company prepared an Environmental Impact Statement when it applied to the local council for rezoning.

The EIS identified the natural and cultural values of the site, and the developers (Queensland Tourism Industries Limited) adopted a number of design and operational guidelines that were in keeping with an overall ecotourism development philosophy. These included:

- undertaking a survey plan to identify and mark all major trees on the site so that roads and buildings could be planned around them;
- limiting the height of all buildings to below the tree line and using natural bush colours for all external finishes;
- using local materials and services as far as possible (more than 95 per cent sourced locally);
- using native species from the site and surrounds in all landscaping (requiring the construction of a large native plant nursery);
- mulching all vegetable material removed from the building site and using it for landscaping;
- limiting the importation of landfill or gravel to disease-free sources, or the island;
- diverting run-off from roads and roofs into lakes to reduce scouring;
- regulating and monitoring contractors over tree clearance and disturbance (fines of up to $1,000 were established for unauthorised tree removal).

Savings on energy have been significant because all options were considered at the planning stage:

- the hotel complex was designed to provide passive cooling as opposed to air conditioning, saving an estimated 500,000 kW/h of energy annually;
- low energy fluorescent lighting uses 15 per cent of normal power consumption;
- the use of a sealed sewage system meant that it could be located near the complex, saving 150,000 kW/h of energy per year in pumping the waste over a sand dune for treatment.

A full time director of environmental management was appointed in 1991 to manage the planning and implementation of the environment of the 65 hectare site.

Many of these initiatives exceeded the legal requirements of the time, but the company's commitment to the ecotourism ethic and the future of the resort through sensitive, sustainable management has created a benchmark for ecotourism development.

Kingfisher Bay Resort and Village has won over 20 international, national, state and regional awards for design and environmental tourism.

Alternatives

The assessment of alternatives can be the most controversial element of an EIA. The developer should evaluate all reasonable alternatives to the proposal, such as using a different site, altering the scale and type of development, and the consequences of "doing nothing". For example, an evaluation of the "do nothing" option in the case of degraded land may show that the site will become worse with no development, whereas some development combined with a program of rehabilitation could be beneficial to the area and the community.

Strategies

The developer needs to outline techniques and strategies to reduce any of the impacts that have been identified and to provide a process of dealing with unforseen issues and emergencies, such as natural disasters or equipment failure. Strategies for education and training may need to be established to deal with social issues.

The developer also needs to make a commitment to implement such strategies, to regulate and monitor the environment — both social and natural. Monitoring must continue after construction, but its extent will depend on the sensitivity of the environment.

Dealing with Building Contractors

Even with a small tourism venture that you are building yourself, you will probably need to use building contractors for some of the construction. It is important to establish environmental guidelines on procedures with them. These may include controls on the destruction of native plants, handling waste materials through re-use and recycling, and restricting the introduction of foreign plant species into a particularly fragile ecosystem. Avoid construction during times of the year when heavy rain or high winds may occur, as the potential for erosion and other damage is increased.

Fines or reduced payment may be introduced for non-compliance, or a performance bond could be collected before the work begins. However, consultation and education are often more effective than "the big stick" approach. A briefing or training session may be the most effective way of explaining your position if you are using large numbers of contractors and staff, as it enables feedback and questions, thus ensuring that the message is received.

Regular monitoring of the site and follow-up sessions on-site with the contractors will keep the environmental priorities uppermost in their minds.

After the rules are in place, it is important that you are easily accessible to solve any problems or confusion that may arise. Construction could be severely delayed while the developers wait for a decision on an unidentified plant they have "discovered".

Integrating Construction and Environment

The construction of the Skyrail gondola cableway in a World Heritage rainforest area of Far North Queensland involved some very strict environmental procedures.

New methods of construction were devised that would incorporate the environmental philosophy of a World Heritage area, and the developers paid a high bond to the land management agency.

The sites of the towers (at a maximum size of 10 square metres) were selected to utilise existing canopy gaps, limiting the need for clearing as much as possible.

Stringent conditions were placed on all survey crews and workmen, including limiting the surveyors' trails to less than one metre wide and prohibiting them from clearing any vegetation larger than a human wrist. All construction staff had to hike to the site of each tower. An inventory was taken of all plant species growing on the tower sites and seeds were collected to be propagated and replanted after construction. Clearing was done by vertical demolition — the branches are lowered piece by piece — so that nothing outside the construction site was damaged. All hand tools and boots were sterilised to ensure that no weeds or foreign plants were introduced to the area.

All on-site workers undertook an intensive induction program that explained the importance of World Heritage values. They were also provided with the Skyrail Code of Environmental Practice and a general instruction book that included rules and practices to be followed by all workers.

All concrete and materials were flown in by helicopter at the end of 300-foot-long lines so that the helicopters could fly high enough to avoid damaging the rainforest through the down draft of the rotor blades.

Marine Development

While the development of marinas and jetties is similar in many ways to construction on land, there are some additional environmental issues to address. These include: establishing procedures to prevent the movement of sediment to levels higher (or lower) than existing levels, establishing treatment procedures for contaminated run-off at the source of the contamination, and maintaining vegetation on the banks of water courses to act as a natural sediment and nutrient filter.

Protective structures such as breakwaters can dramatically alter wave action and tidal flow as well as affecting marine life, so it is important that good water exchange is maintained in all tidal conditions, including low tide. The same protective structures must be able to withstand damage from storms, and pressure from currents and waves.

The design stage of marina development is extremely important, and plans for efficient effluent disposal must be included at this stage. Onshore facilities such as car and trailer parking, toilets, and information centres need to be environmentally sensitive as they will often be constructed on sandy areas.

Construction of Access Routes, Tracks and Boardwalks

To minimise the high risk of increased water run-off or channelling whenever any type of track, road or access route is constructed, a number of basic criteria should be followed.

If the ground is sloping, follow the contours to minimise the gradient, and avoid areas with steep slopes or those that require extensive cutting and filling. All slopes and banks will need to be stabilised, preferably with native plants, but some other material may be needed, particularly in the short term while the plants are getting established. Crossing or damming gullies and streams will alter the flow of water and should be avoided, as should travelling to a dead-end which could become a fire trap.

Visual impacts are also important and can be minimised by landscaping along road and track verges, using run-off water for the plants. Car parks, service and storage areas also should be screened with native vegetation to enhance the visual aspect.

Boardwalks

Boardwalks are increasing in popularity as an alternative to compacted tracks. They not only minimise trampling and erosion but are extremely effective in channelling visitor movements and type of use.

Technical and building approaches are continually being developed and improved as each environment offers its own individual challenges. For example, at Maits Rest in Victoria, the developers devised a technique which required only half the number of supports normally used for the boardwalk, thus reducing interference with the forest floor. At Shark Bay in Western Australia, the gauge and placement of decking over the stromatolites had to admit enough light to enable the marine creatures to survive, without affecting the safety of visitors. This also required the development of innovative technology.

Energy

The greatest opportunities to save energy costs and minimise usage are during the design and construction phases of a development. Developers can either take a long-term, integrated view of energy efficiency or adapt existing buildings. The latter approach can incur greater costs and less efficiency, though it is still worth considering. Energy-saving devices, both passive and active, and renewable energy sources (sources not depleted by their use) such as solar, wind and water, are most effective when incorporated into the original design of a building, or when refurbishing and replacing.

The cost of renewable energy and energy-efficient technology is often regarded as high, with a limited financial return, and so only within the reach of those who can afford to "feel good about the environment". In general, these alternative technologies do cost more to buy than conventional systems, but they last longer and are cheaper to run, thus paying for the initial set-up costs.

It is important to seek quality, expert advice when considering your energy requirements and the range of options available. Appendix Three contains contact details of some energy groups and associations that could help.

General Efficiency

Different models of appliances (especially refrigerators and televisions) vary greatly in the amount of energy they consume even for the same sized appliance, so it is important to find out what their energy use is. All electric appliances these days display an energy rating — make sure that you understand these ratings and how they apply to your needs. Information is available from your local electricity supplier or from the Commonwealth Department of Primary Industries and Energy (contact details in Appendix Three).

The energy use of conventional refrigeration appliances and some energy efficient appliances is compared below (this descriptive example is not intended to promote any particular product, so brand names are not used). This simple example indicates that about 1,800 watts per day can be saved using energy-efficient refrigeration.

	Conventional Appliances			Efficient Appliances		
	230 litre refrig.	230 litre freezer	total	230 litre refrig.	230 litre freezer	total
Power (watts)	260	130		100	100	
Daily Operation(hours)	9	12		9	12	
Daily Load	2340	1560	3,900	900	1200	2,100

Source: Department of Industry, Science and Tourism, "Tourism Switched On"

In most cases, leaving appliances on will consume additional energy. One way to ensure that appliances are turned off when a room is empty is to make guests use a key tag in a master switch for the room or unit, so that when they leave and take their key with them, the power to selected appliances is disconnected.

Lighting

When considering lighting requirements, remember that dark, textured walls, which may provide an intimate atmosphere, can also absorb up to 90 per cent of light. Light coloured walls on the other hand reflect about the same amount, greatly increasing the lighting of an area. This also applies to lamp-shades and reflectors. Desk lights and lower background lighting can save energy, while dirty light covers can reduce light output by up to 50 per cent.

High efficiency, low energy light globes use about one-fifth the electricity of normal globes, however they take a few minutes to "warm up" and reach full brightness. Their life is shortened if they are constantly turned on and off but they are excellent for public lighting areas such as lounges, outdoor areas and hallways. Fluorescent lights can be even more efficient than some low voltage lights, and take less time to reach full brightness, however they also suffer from constant turning on and off. If using fluorescent tubes, triphosphor tubes provide more light per watt and a better colour than the standard ones.

Skylights can be effective in increasing natural light and are a popular source of passive lighting, but they are often poorly insulated, resulting in unwanted heat loss or gain. Skylights without these problems are available and careful design, selection and use should help.

Insulation

If the building envelope is adequately insulated, the energy required for heating or cooling is greatly reduced. Insulation is best done during the construction phase as, apart from the roof cavity, areas (such as in between the walls) are not easy to access in existing buildings. Materials used in insulation include fibrous materials (like fibreglass, natural wool, and polyester fibre), foam, and recycled materials such as newspapers that have been treated with a fire retardant.

As well as retaining warmth or coolness, insulation reduces noise transfer through walls and ceilings, a particular benefit for tourism accommodation where most people prefer privacy and as little noise from the neighbours as possible. Whilst this is not a direct environmental benefit, it can certainly be a social one!

The most difficult areas to insulate are windows, as glass allows heat to travel easily both ways. Installing close fitting curtains will cut the transfer rate by up to 50 per cent, and double glazing will also halve heat loss and sound transfer. Insulated shutters can be closed at night or even during the day when the room is unoccupied.

Passive Solar Heating and Cooling

Solar power is one of the most common sources of renewable energy, and the opportunities for using the sun to cool and heat living spaces, water and swimming pools are many and varied.

A new building can be designed to take advantage of natural sunlight and airflow, through its siting and by using materials that collect, store and distribute solar energy. Heating from the sun's rays can be combined with a thermal mass that stores the daytime heat from the sun for release in the evening. The simplest method is having windows facing the sun (generally north in the southern hemisphere) with concrete slab floors and internal brick walls acting as the thermal mass. With existing structures, sun spaces, such as external glass houses and atriums, can be added.

Where large windows would cause a loss of privacy, or lose too much internal heat in extremely cold climates, such as the snow fields (even with insulation), a Trombe wall can be built. A brick wall behind a glass window is heated by the sun during the day, and releases the heat into the living area at night.

In warmer climates, the sun can actually be used to help cool buildings. By constructing a raised section of roof, it can act as a "solar chimney" when heated, drawing fresh air from a shaded area such as the basement or garden through the building, and creating a breeze. Applied in conjunction with other design features that keep direct sun off the building, such as verandas, overhangs and shutters, this type of cooling can be extremely effective and virtually maintenance and cost free. To assist the natural flow of air throughout a building, incorporate smaller, lower openings on the breeze side and larger ones on the side away from it.

In climates that are warm both day and night, concrete floors and brick walls (which act as thermal mass) may not be the best choice — a well-shaded weatherboard building will respond quickly to temperature changes, allowing the building to cool down quickly with slight changes in temperature.

Natural Air Conditioning

Coconut Beach Resort in Far North Queensland has designed its units to use natural cross-ventilation and shading from the tropical rainforest trees in place of noisy air conditioners. The open architecture enhances the resort's nature-based image, and the quiet allows visitors to enjoy the surrounding natural environment. The operators of the resort have spent some time "educating" inbound tour operators so they do not bring visitors straight from a cold, northern hemisphere climate to the tropics without allowing some time to acclimatise. By doing this, the international tourists are not as likely to suffer from the sudden heat and demand air conditioning.

Solar Panels

Using solar panels as the primary source of water heating, with a supplementary energy source (gas, oil, electricity) for cloudy days, can provide both cost and environmental benefits. The most effective solar panels have selective coatings that absorb visible light, but do not radiate much heat back, increasing the temperatures that can be reached in the system.

Couran Cove — an Ecotourism Resort

Couran Cove Resort on South Stradbroke Island, off Queensland's Gold Coast is an interesting study in the development of a large-scale resort along ecotourism lines. Original plans for the site, some 20 years ago, included a Gold Coast style city with a simulated Hawaiian village, the mandatory golf course, and a marina with an extensive canal system.

The current developer, Interpacific Resorts bought the Couran Cove Resort site in 1990. While the development is still large scale and by its very nature will have impacts on the environment, Interpacific has committed to developing a nature-based resort with associated activities and management practices, including restoration of degraded areas. The developers recognise that the resort's appeal will lie in the environmental experience. The development plans exceed current Queensland environmental regulations and a number of best practice models are being established.

The 68 hectare resort extends from the Boardwater in the west to the surf beach in the east, encompassing a range of environments from dry banksia and wattle scrub to melaleuca woodlands and a Liverstona palm forest. In the past, the sand dunes were mined but most have been revegetated and established.

Accommodation and resort facilities will include a convention centre, 192 marine apartments and 50 lagoon lodges to be built around the previously constructed canal and lagoon system. A second stage includes 300 ecocabins to be built in the bush, providing a high level of individual privacy. Guest facilities include a swimming pool, gymnasium, spas and massage huts, tennis and squash courts and an interpretive and research centre.

Building design will incorporate passive design techniques providing solar cooling, heating and lighting.

Environmental Impact Minimisation

An early problem for the developers during construction was the disturbance of potential acid sulphate soils. These soils, currently beneath the water table, may oxidise when exposed to the air and cause acidic runoff. This in turn would kill fish and destroy water habitat so they must be treated with great care. A management strategy was developed to handle the soil, which involves separating materials under water and covering the suspect material with sand so it is never brought to the surface and exposed.

During the design stage, all vegetation and significant trees were identified and mapped, and the resort designed around the natural vegetation. The long-term effects of earthworks were analysed and designs were developed to minimise impacts on existing vegetation.

Water Management

When assessing the fresh water supply needs of the resort, the developers considered the whole issue of water management, including supply and treatment, sewage treatment and stormwater collection and disposal, resulting in an integrated water management strategy. Some of the measures adopted include:
- appliances using limited potable water (thus conserving it for human consumption)
- use of endemic vegetation to minimise water irrigation

- collection of rainwater for toilet flushing
- on-site tertiary sewage treatment and re-use of sewage effluent for irrigation

Power

The major power source for the resort is a gas lined power generator. This was chosen over a diesel generator due to the relatively clean exhaust and greater capacity for waste heat recovery. The waste heat will be used to heat water, both for direct human use as well as pool heating. Waste oil will also be recycled.

Solar power will be used in conjunction with the generated power in all of the lodges and eco-cabins.

Visitor Education and Staff Training

An education, research and interpretation centre will be an integral part of the development, and staff will be trained in relation to the company's environmental management plan.

The interpretation centre will incorporate the rich cultural heritage of the area (indigenous and non-indigenous) as well as the environment.

Consultation

The developers have worked closely with state and local government at all stages, ensuring that requirements are being met, and in many cases exceeded, for example, developing the area less intensively than allowed. Local environmental and other interest groups have been consulted in the planning stages as well as throughout the development. This provided constructive input into the development, with many recommendations being included in the plan.

Couran Cove has the potential to be another working example of ecotourism best practice in Australia.

For heating swimming pools, a different type of solar heater is required due to the chlorine or salt content in the pool. They are often made of plastic pipe and spread over a large area such as a roof. These collectors can raise the temperature of a pool by four or five degrees Celsius. Pools should be covered with insulated material when they are not being used to avoid losing the heat through evaporative and convective cooling.

Utilising the design techniques described above is described as "passive" solar design. If constructing a new building, the use of a design specialist is recommended, as there are many factors to be considered in developing an efficient design that will suit your needs. The savings in the power bill will soon pay for the designer.

Electricity

For various reasons (excessive environmental damage, economics, ethical preferences or remoteness) it is not always possible for a business to be connected to an electricity grid, so energy must be supplied on-site. The conventional approach is to use diesel powered generators, but their inefficiency results in expensive electricity.

The alternative is to use renewable energy sources linked to an array of batteries, with the diesel (or petrol) generator being used only as a back-up. Renewable power technology includes photovoltaic cells, wind turbines and micro-hydro electric schemes. Often a combination is used to maintain the power supply.

Photovoltaics (Solar Energy)

Photovoltaic cells convert sunlight into electricity which is stored in a bank of batteries. They can be used in most areas of Australia and the New Zealand North Island due to the availability of sunlight all year round — even cloudy days provide significant solar radiation. As the cells are expensive, the system should be matched closely with the needs of the development. Although the cost of photovoltaic cells is falling, it generally takes ten to fifteen years to recover their higher initial capital costs through lower running costs.

However, smaller photovoltaic systems are relatively cheap and are being used for outdoor lighting, electric fences, barbeques (in many national parks) or communication links, such as remote area telephones and radio transmission towers. Photovoltaic systems are also used to operate fans for composting toilets, enabling them to be used in remote locations. (Composting toilets are discussed later in this chapter.)

Where the development can be connected to the electricity grid, excess power can be sold to the commercial power utility (which, in effect, stores it) and bought back as and when it is needed. Often power would be exported to the grid during the day when the sun is out and taken from the grid at night when there is greater demand and no actual solar production.

Photovoltaic panels can be incorporated into the design of buildings or retrofitted to existing buildings. They can be part of the roof of a building or carport, provide additional sun shading in glass domes or fixed awnings, form facade cladding, and contained in skylights and sun spaces. Some of the smaller systems are mounted on poles, particularly when used for remote appliances such as outdoor lighting.

The panels can be mounted on a horizontal plane (such as a flat roof), tilted towards the sun, adjusted to counteract the seasonal movement of the sun, or set on solar tracking rigs that follow the sun from dawn to dusk. Solar tracking gains 25–40 per cent more energy than non-tracking units.

Typical tourism operations using photovoltaics are island resorts, outback and rural accommodation providers, and wilderness tourism operators, as well as those with ethical reasons to use renewable energy.

Wind Turbines

At exposed, windy sites a wind turbine may prove to be more economical than solar cells. Their effectiveness depends primarily on wind speed, with a doubling of the speed producing an eight-fold increase in electricity. Consequently, before deciding to invest in this form of renewable energy, it would be wise to find out the average wind speeds for the whole year. An annual average wind speed of at least 20 km per hour would be suitable

The most common turbine design has one, two or three blades and mounted on a tower to gain maximum wind advantage, it looks much like a traditional farming windmill. While traditional windmills are used primarily to pump water, wind turbines have been developed to turn a great deal faster to produce electricity. Another efficient turbine design is the "catenary", which is shaped like an egg-beater on a vertical pole, however it does not withstand strong winds and requires more maintenance than other designs.

Electricity produced by turbines can be stored in a bank of batteries or sold to the electricity grid. Due to the number of batteries required to store electricity and the capacity of generators to produce it, selling electricity to the grid can be a convenient and cost-effective means of storage.

Generating Energy on an Island

Many islands, due to their remoteness, have had to develop their own energy production systems. These places provide excellent case studies. Tortoise Head Guest House is on French Island in Victoria's Western Port Bay. Although it is not far from the mainland, it is remote in terms of access and facilities. Catering for up to 28 guests, it is powered by an integrated range of sources, including a wind turbine, photovoltaic system and back-up diesel generator. As the guest house is not connected to the grid, it maintains a large bank of batteries (20 six-volt batteries).

Because their power needs rely on nature, the owners have found that they must adjust their energy use and associated living patterns to suit the conditions. For example, they use equipment with greater energy demands (such as computers and washing machines) on windy days and carefully budget their energy use on calm days. The combination of energy sources and the back-up generator does, however, provide them with sufficient power to meet guests' expectations of being able to use personal appliances (mainly hair dryers) regardless of the conditions. There are some things that tourists will not go without!

Micro-Hydro

Micro-hydro systems use falling water to drive a turbine that produces electricity. They do not require vast amounts of water, but can utilise quite small stream, depending on the water pressure and flow rate — greater water pressure will reduce the flow rate needed.

Micro-hydro systems offer an excellent renewable energy choice where solar or wind power generation is not possible, such as in forested, sheltered and shady areas. They are not reliant on seasonal factors (except in dry areas) so it is possible to generate power 24 hours per day, all year round. The systems are also reliable and require minimal maintenance, even when run full-time, so the initial high outlay is soon recovered.

Typical tourism users of this technology may include resorts in mountainous areas and any place where there is a permanent supply of running water. Micro-hydros can still be used where the supply of water is not reliable or is only small if the demand for power is intermittent and low. For example, cabins that are only used for a few days at a time may have enough power stored in the battery bank and time to recharge between visits.

It is important to consider the environmental and social implications of using a stream or river to produce your electricity. Insensitive earthworks that may create erosion, or excessive water use resulting in stream flow reduction (or even cessation) will affect not only the environment, but also downstream users. Correct environmental planning is crucial, and, as with all these technologies, an appropriately qualified designer/engineer should be consulted.

Co-generation and Waste Heat Recovery

Heat is a by-product of electricity production, so any system that is generating electricity on-site releases heat into the atmosphere. By using a co-generation system, this wasted heat could be used to provide heating for water (including swimming pools) and space heating, as well as cooling with absorption chillers. This type of system has a turbine or engine that drives the generator, and the waste heat is collected and utilised as it is produced. Co-generation is especially suited to situations where there is a high demand for heat at the same time that electricity is being produced, as storing heat can be expensive and impractical — which is why it has been let go as waste in so many situations.

Its suitability for hotels and resorts with continual power and heating requirements has been recognised in Europe, but not many Australian or New Zealand tourism enterprises have adopted co-generation. The main users have been large scale industries such as sugar refineries and mineral processing plants. However, there is no reason why it should not be used by other industries, and tourism operators are starting to pay attention and incorporate aspects of waste heat recovery in the design of their properties.

Other waste heat, such as that generated from the cooling coils of refrigerators, freezers and air conditioners, can also be utilised in a constructive way.

> ## Heating the Green Island Swimming Pool
>
> Another island resort that generates its own electricity is Green Island, near Cairns in Far North Queensland.
>
> The water used to cool the generator engines collects the waste heat, and is heated up to 80 degrees Celsius. This water is circulated through a heat exchanger that in turn heats the water in the swimming pool. By utilising the power generation by-product of heat in this way, the amount of heating fuel to be transported from the mainland has been reduced.

Biomass Combustion

The burning of "biofuels", that is fuel produced from plants and animals (wood, organic and biological waste), as opposed to the fossil fuel group (coal, petroleum, diesel and natural gas) is described as biomass combustion. Many efficient and clean burning appliances, such as heating furnaces for water or air and wood-burning heaters for single rooms, are now available. In many areas, firewood is cheaper than oil, gas or electricity and the visible flame and glowing coals provide an ambient atmosphere that visitors enjoy.

However, there are environmental concerns regarding the use of firewood, and it is important to check the source to make sure that no environmental damage is occurring from its collection. Good sources of firewood include waste wood from clearing or routine forest management, or your own woodlot. Establishing a small woodlot can be done effectively and relatively quickly by using highly productive coppice techniques and irrigating with water from your sewage system after secondary treatment.

Wood is not the only biofuel that you can use. While much animal waste is difficult to handle and may smell, there are other alternatives. Briquettes are

> ## Boosting Heating Capacity
>
> Seven Oaks Country Gardens and Retreat, in the Strzelecki Ranges, Victoria, comprises a large rambling country house and three separate guest cottages. Renewable energy sources are used for heat and power, while heating and cooking energy is provided by wood grown on the property and solar and wind used to generate electricity.
>
> As the needs of the operation could not be met by existing combustion stoves and heaters, the owners contracted a biomass specialist to design the wood burning stoves to their specifications. The stove in the main house is large enough to cook for ten people, and heat both a standard hot water service and water for central heating. The second stove provides space heating and hot water to the cabins.

made from dry organic material placed under high pressure to form solid bricks and have a similar volatility to wood. They are commercially available, and even used newspapers can be used to make briquettes, however the process takes a few months. Wood need not be the only fuel grown in a woodlot. Sugar cane and oil crops (such as sunflowers, soya, linseed etc.) may be used as fuel. After pressing them to retrieve their oil (or sugar) the pulp can be burnt as fuel.

Methane and other gases created from landfill and agricultural waste are also being used as sources of energy that can be burnt to provide electricity.

Many of the materials mentioned above are part of a farmer's life, so if you are located near a farm or run one yourself, the use of biofuels should be considered. Many farming communities have been using them for generations.

Minimising Energy Use in Day-to-Day Operations

As well as using products that require less power, energy use can be minimised by altering the way things are done, that is by avoiding the need to consume energy as well as being energy efficient. This may mean changing habits that have been developed over a lifetime, but the effort is often worth the results of saving money and energy.

Pumping Water

Where it is necessary to pump water, selecting the correct sized pump and motor will avoid the problems associated with inefficient pumping (if it is too small) and extra costs (if it is too large). Where the loads vary, a variable speed drive will improve the pump's efficiency at minimal cost.

If pumping to a water tank, a float switch in the tank that switches the pump off when it is full will avoid over-use and prevent water overflowing and causing soil erosion. Wherever possible, arrange the piping so that water is delivered to the point of use without having to be re-pressurised.

Hot Water Usage

Heating water by traditional electric means generates about half the greenhouse emissions of the accommodation sector, so any reduction will benefit the environment. Prevent hot water drips and leaks by regularly checking tap washers, and encourage both staff and guests to conserve hot water by filling electric (or gas) kettles from the cold tap and rinsing dishes in cold water.

The use of renewable energy sources and co-generation will reduce the need for commercial, coal-produced electricity.

Regardless of the energy source, losses of heat can, and should be, limited by installing extra insulation around heat storage tanks and pipes. Water should be heated to between 55 and 60 degrees Celsius, so if the hot water service is heating water above this alter the thermostat, which will save on power and heat loss.

Cooking

Microwave and induction cooking are more efficient than conventional electric hotplates, while gas (including LPG) has less environmental impact. Keeping food hot uses a lot of energy, so minimising the time it needs to be heated and keeping it in insulated, closed containers will save energy. Good cooking practices include keeping lids on pots and using the lowest suitable cooking settings on appliances. Also, careful selection of items on a menu can limit the variety of cooking equipment used for a meal, with salads and quick to prepare meals minimising cooking energy.

In commercial kitchens, appliances are often kept on in case they are needed. By selecting equipment that quickly reaches operational condition, it can be turned off until actually required.

Refrigeration

Just as operating hot water services at too high a temperature increases unnecessary energy use, running refrigeration equipment too cold can increase both energy use and running costs — a refrigerator that is one degree too cold can cost five per cent more to run. Door seals prevent the leakage of cold air, and it is important to keep them clean and make sure that doors shut properly.

Non-perishables such as soft drinks do not need to refrigerated until a few hours before they are needed, however keep them in a cool place so that less energy is required to cool them.

Correct installation of refrigeration systems is crucial to their efficient operation, and allowance must be made for good ventilation around the coils at the back. For example, bar fridges that have been installed in cabinets without suitable ventilation can cost up to one and a half times more to operate — inlet and outlet slots need to be cut into the cabinet. Locating refrigerators near hot equipment such as stoves or in direct sunlight will also increase the amount of energy required.

If you have airconditioning, simultaneously running a ceiling fan will reduce the energy required for cooling. The fan provides comfort at warmer temperatures, so the air conditioner need not be set as low as when it is operating alone. If the fan is solar powered, it can make even greater reductions.

Washing and Drying

One load of clothes washing can use up to 200 litres of water, one third of which may be heated, so both the operation of the machine and the heating of water can use large amounts of energy. By encouraging guests to use towels and linen for more than one day, and fully loading washing machines, the number of loads will be reduced. Washing in cold water whenever possible will also save energy.

Front loading washing machines use less water and detergent and are gentler on clothes (good for prolonging the life of towels and linen). Washing machines with a spin speed of at least 1,000 rpm will reduce the drying time and energy required. Use clothes lines to dry clothes wherever possible as they utilise solar and wind energy, and even in wet climates clothes will often be dried by the wind if they are under cover. Waste heat can be used for dryers and drying rooms, which, if situated behind fire places or refrigeration systems, make direct use of the heat without having to transport it.

Before washing dishes, scrape food off plates and if rinsing is required, use cold water. Washing in a domestic sink uses about 15 litres of water and a commercial sink 40 litres, whereas an efficient dishwasher can use as little as 15 litres with a far greater load. Dishwashers should be fully loaded and packed efficiently so that they are used effectively.

Facilities for drying hands range from paper towels to electric hand dryers and continuous roll cloth towels, all of which have varying environmental impacts. Recycled paper towels are preferable to non-recycled, and electric hand dryers with a movement sensor to turn them on and off are preferable to push button timers as they are only in use when hands are actually being dried. Continuous roll cloth requires careful laundering, so unless washing is handled in a low-impact manner it may not be a good environmental option.

In all of the washing cases outlined above, try to use non-phosphorous detergents as the phosphorus compounds in many products contribute to environmental problems such as algal bloom. Some cleaning products are not compatible with some waste systems, so it is advisable to check the requirements of your system before using any cleaners.

Office Equipment

A desktop computer can cost about $100 per annum to run if it is on most of the time, whereas laptop computers use about one tenth of the energy. If a computer needs to stay on to receive data or act as a file server, turn off the screen, which uses the most energy. Laser printers have great quality but require a lot of energy, whereas the inkjet style printers use much less. You can save paper by using the double-sided capability of photocopiers.

Paper can also be reduced by using electronic storage and transfer — email is a form of electronic communication that is becoming extremely popular around the world, and faxes can be sent direct from a computer without being printed out. Purchase and use recycled paper and re-use office paper if it is only printed on one-side, before recycling it. On-site recycling can be done by mulching and composting paper.

Many printers and photocopiers can use recycled paper and have ink cartridges that can be refilled rather than discarded when they run out. The number of manufacturers who will accept old equipment for recycling is increasing, so patronise these manufacturers if the rest of their energy requirements are satisfactory.

Waste Minimisation

Reducing the amount of waste that is created and handling it correctly is extremely important for the environment. While waste management is a high priority in cities, it is an even greater one in country areas as many sensitive natural areas are nearby. A business involved in ecotourism is even more likely to be situated near such areas, which may or may not have the protection of national park or World Heritage listing. Even those areas with such protection are vulnerable to what goes on nearby, outside the area of protection. Facilities near national parks or other environments must ensure their wastes are unable escape and affect the park's ecosystems.

Setting waste management priorities can sometimes conflict with the perceptions of tourists, many of whom may consider themselves environmentally aware, but have a limited knowledge of the extent and true value of good environmental practices. They may recognise the importance of minimising packaging to reduce rubbish, which is a visible waste product, but show less interest in less visible — but more important —waste management areas such as grey water handling. Effective waste management procedures may have an impact on the quality and expectations of the tourism experience, which in turn could affect client satisfaction and the economic viability of the business. These issues must be considered when developing waste management priorities and techniques, and often an education program is required to improve visitors' understanding and acceptance.

Reducing Waste

By looking at records of what, and how many, goods are being purchased (newspapers, processed and fresh food, fresh water) and comparing them with the amount and type of waste that is being produced (waste paper, grey water, sewage, food scraps) you can see which areas contribute most to your waste. It also provides a comparison when examining the effectiveness of waste management measures that have been introduced.

Some general strategies that will reduce waste include purchasing food and other materials in bulk to reduce packaging and avoiding over-packaged items. But be careful not to over-order and make sure you have adequate, energy-efficient storage facilities. There are many ways of minimising food wastage — from portion control and pre-ordering of meals to self service, as well as good storage facilities. Introducing dispensers for coffee, sugar, soap and shampoo (as opposed to individual single serves) is a visible way to reduce packaging which many tourists regard favourably. Using water-efficient appliances reduces waste (grey) water, and cooking without fats or oils is not only healthy for the environment but also for people. Dry composting toilets dramatically reduce the volume of waste water and sewage effluent.

Re-using and Recycling

Using materials more than once reduces not only the volume of waste, but also the consumption of resources by limiting the demand for high quantities of a product. Some items, such as mugs, containers, plates and utensils, can be re-used for the same purpose. Always avoid disposable items like paper plates. Other items can be re-used for a different purpose, for example, grey water used to water gardens and newspaper used for fuel.

Many local governments collect goods for recycling, including aluminium, glass, plastic and newspaper. Many local garages recycle tyres and oil and other manufacturers will take back old equipment for recycling.

Re-use is even better than recycling which can be associated with high energy costs of transport and reprocessing, especially in country areas where recycling infrastructure is not as prevalent as in cities. However, tourists generally believe that recycling is the best option, probably because their municipal councils actively encouraging recycling and undertake mass educational programs. Some island resorts handle their own recycling programs, but they are still limited by their own energy concerns and limitations. By purchasing goods made from recycled materials, demand for them will increase and recycling infrastructure will eventually improve.

Organic wastes can be composted on-site and used as a soil conditioner, worm farms convert organic and paper waste into vermicast (worm droppings) and waste water can be recycled and used to water gardens. There are many composting systems on the market which are simple and yield no odour or insect problems.

Building Materials

Many of the materials used for construction can cause environmental damage, and any tourist development must consider reducing these components. Re-using old buildings or second-hand building materials can reduce the demand for new resources, and an increasing number of construction materials are being made from wastes such as plastic, paper and scrap wood. The use of materials that are either waste or surplus to their traditional use is increasing, with many innovators working in this field.

If you are using building contractors, ask them to provide a waste minimisation plan which includes guarantees and compensation for failing to meet certain standards. Local government will be able to advise you about what should be included in these contracts and may even be able to recommend contractors who have a good environmental record.

Accurate estimate of materials is important to avoid the economic and environmental costs of over-ordering. Identify ways that left-over materials can be re-used or recycled by looking for suppliers who will take back any unused material; alternatively, you may be able to sell surplus materials.

Sewage

If there is no centralised sewage system, (the situation at most ecotourism sites) waste water can be the most damaging emission from a tourist complex. (Waste water includes "grey" water from showers, kitchens and laundries and "black" water from toilets.) Handling and disposal of sewage is a major environmental and hygiene concern. The nutrients contained in solid human waste and the large amount of contaminated water released by toilets can damage sensitive ecosystems.

If you are connected to a sewage system, a number of options are available to reduce water needs. By using low volume, dual flush systems (typically, six litre/three litre systems) or ultra low flush systems that use less than two litres per flush, the amount of water required is dramatically reduced. Also, water from roof run-off can be collected and used for water flushing, reducing the requirements placed on other fresh water sources. To minimise the range of contaminants in the used water, reduce the use of chemical cleaners and deodorants in the toilet water and use only those that break down quickly.

Where there is no sewage system, the options for waste water treatment include the use of septic tanks, drainage pipes into leach areas, evaporation ponds, activated sludge systems and artificial wetlands or reed beds that use aquatic plants to remove pollutants. These artificial wetlands can also be a landscaping feature of a resort and act as a highly visual indicator of the company's environmental commitment. A further option is the use of composting toilets.

Composting, (dry conservancy) toilets do not require water for flushing as they rely on the waste composting in the toilet structure itself. They are particularly suited to areas where water is scarce, they reduce the bulk of the waste, and produce a high nutrient compost.

Composting toilets operate on the principle of aerobically composting organic waste. They require a flow through of oxygen and a moisture content of less than 60 per cent. In order to achieve this, a solar-powered fan and passive solar energy draw air into the composting drum and circulate it. The warm air reduces the moisture content and accelerates the composting process. The humus collected in the composting drum is so compact that it may need to be removed only every few months.

However, customers and staff need to be educated about the use and benefits of the system, and cultural and social considerations need to be taken into account. Many people are reluctant to change their toilet habits, and all societies have certain taboos regarding defecation. Consultation with staff and potential users will highlight some of these issues, but ongoing support and education is also required. Usually, if the system is well maintained and air-flow is kept at levels that allow odourless aerobic composting — as opposed to the odorous anaerobic composting used in septic systems — there should be little customer resistance to dry composting toilets.

The other major sewage problem is the disposal of oils and fats, which often end up as untreated sewage with a great potential to damage the environment. Grease filters on sinks and grease traps in larger kitchens should be used before any waste is discharged. Grease traps utilise the natural separation of grease and water to separate the liquids which can be disposed of normally. The grease should be disposed of according to the state/territory environmental protection authority and local water board requirements.

Oils and fats can also be removed from crockery with absorbent towels, and cooking oils can be re-used a number of times.

Composting Toilets a Viable Option

Jemby-Rinjah Lodge in the Blue Mountains of New South Wales, is an owner-operated 100 bed ecotourism venture on the boundary of a national park. Accommodation is provided in self-contained cabins and larger eco-lodges, which use composting toilets. During the cold winter when solar heating is low, warm air from inside the heated living area is used to reduce the moisture content and promote biological activity. The solid, dried wastes from the toilet are combined with organic waste, further composted, and used as garden fertiliser.

The toilets are cleaned using an enzyme based cleaner which also assists in the composting process and is constantly fed into the toilet bowl.

The use of composting toilets and enzyme based cleaners means there is no danger of effluent impacting on the ecosystem of the national park.

The NSW Department of Health permitted the original trial and evaluation of composting toilets at Jemby-Rinjah, and has now licensed them for residential and commercial use.

Water Conservation

Water is one of the most highly used (and at times, abused) resources in this country. Many of the environmental practices and technologies discussed in this chapter relate to the conservation of water, such as the dry composting toilets, as toilet flushings account for one-third of our water use. The less water that is used will reduce the amount of waste water to be cleaned up, which will in turn reduce treatment costs.

Each guest in a standard hotel uses between 100 and 300 cubic metres of water annually. A reasonable goal would be 100 litres per day, which is only 40 cubic metres per year. Reduced toilet flushing through the introduction of dual flush or composting systems and using front loading washing machines (that require about half of the water of top-loading machines) will reduce daily water consumption dramatically.

Water-efficient shower heads can also reduce the amount of water used, but it is important to get a shower head that will be acceptable to your guests — a thin, sharp spray may use less water but it does not cover the body and many people would not like it. A better choice would be a shower head that operates by aerating the water, which reduces water flow and improves wetting. Many different models are available, so test them first to make sure you get what your customers want. Price is not always a guarantee of quality, with some of the cheaper ones being among the most effective. Also, inspect bathrooms for excessive air movement in the room which will cause the water to evaporate quicker, cooling a person's body and thus causing some discomfort.

If you wish to keep your existing shower heads, installing a flow control washer or disc at a very minimal cost of a few dollars each, will reduce the flow from the standard 18 to 24 litres per minute to a more acceptable six, nine or 12 litres per minute.

Leaking taps can waste vast amounts of water, so regularly inspect all taps and install long-lasting washers in them. To prevent taps from being left running, you could install spring-loaded taps, but although these are generally accepted in public facilities your guests may consider them an unnecessary imposition on their comfort. Educating them about the limited water supply may be preferable.

European gardens require a great deal of water, particularly in the warmer, drier Australian climate, and it is suggested that, particularly for ecotourism ventures, native plants endemic to the area be used. They will thrive with minimal attention and encourage native fauna as well.

However, historical gardens may need to be maintained for their cultural heritage, so following a few basic rules will help reduce water consumption. Cover all garden beds with a generous layer of mulch and during the dry times water deeply twice weekly rather than short watering every day. Water early in the morning, late in the evening, or even at night, whichever suits your business and visitors best. If you water during the day, much of the water will evaporate and the more delicate plants may be burnt. Hardier plants can be used to form windbreaks and provide shade for the more delicate species, and keeping lawns long will protect the soil from direct sun.

Environmental Ethics and Regulations

Although environmental regulations differ from state to state, owners or managers of a tourist operation who allow the environment to be damaged can be taken to court. Whether this damage is intentional or not is irrelevant — ignorance of the regulations is not an acceptable defence. Therefore, it is important that you contact your state Environmental Protection Authority (details in Appendix Three) and local council for all relevant information.

To have a sustainable tourism enterprise, it is important to aim for minimal impact, which may go beyond the standards contained in local regulations. All ecotourism operators should be examples of best practice environmental tourism.

As well as avoiding environmental damage, you must be able to demonstrate a commitment to reducing the environmental impact of your business. A plan for dealing with any environmental problems that might arise, such as toxic material leaking into a river or abnormally hot weather creating additional pressure on the water supply is also necessary. Developing an environmental plan that staff can refer to and use will demonstrate your commitment to and understanding of the environment.

Environmental Plan

New developments can start from scratch when developing an environmental plan, and use their Environmental Impact Assessment as the starting point of their planning. The first step for existing operations is to assess their performance, by conducting environmental audits such as an energy and waste self audit.

Energy and Waste Self Audit

Environmental audits can be used to assess a business's environmental performance in terms of its buildings, operations and activities and provide ongoing monitoring in these areas. The individual determines the level of detail of the audit (unless it is required by local legislation or to gain a permit), which can be quite complex, so an energy and waste management professional may need to be consulted.

Such self-audits demonstrate the diligence and commitment of owners towards minimising their impacts on the environment, particularly through energy and waste systems.

A simple audit would include the following areas:

Waste

1 List the type and quantity of waste produced by your operation. Types of waste that should be identified include liquid waste, solid waste (organic and non-organic), gas or heat, and hazardous waste such as chemicals.
2 For each of the waste products identified, list their sources, such as coming from food, fuel, paper, equipment, or cleaning products. Also identify how each waste product came to be at the site, if it was produced as a result of your operation and if it was produced by your staff or visitors.
3 Estimate the cost of this waste, including indirect costs such as the labour cost of removal, running costs for vehicles and tip fees. This information should be readily obtainable from your records.
4 Identify ways of improving the use and disposal of waste by reducing the need for the item in the first place, exploring alternatives, or re-use and recycle.
5 Set targets and develop an action plan.

Energy

1 Identify the types of energy currently being used and whether they are renewable or not.
2 Identify the cost of the energy by checking bills and the cost of appliances.
3 Identify important seasonal trends by putting energy consumption and costs on a graph.
4 Identify the sources of energy consumption by activity and time of day (such as dinner preparation time, night time entertainment, mornings etc) by regularly reading electricity and gas meters.
5 Identify ways of improving the energy use or changing the source to a more environmentally sound one.
6 Set targets and develop an action plan.

Natural Resource Conservation

As well as minimising waste and maximising energy use, it is crucial to conserve the natural environment. Many activities have the potential to degrade the environment through trampling of flora, introducing weeds, removing ground cover or topsoil, compacting the soil, and erosion.

An audit of the activities you offer on your tour or at your property/attraction should also be undertaken. By identifying the range of impacts that the activity may cause, the actual causes can be found and procedures to minimise or eliminate them developed.

For example, if you offer canoeing, an activity audit may include the following points:

1 Identify impacts
   a) erosion of access tracks
   b) erosion of river bank at entry and departure points
   c) introduction of weeds
2 Identify causes (only one cause for each impact is shown, but there will often be more than one cause)
   a) access tracks eroded by heavy use of support vehicles
   b) entry point is on a soft river bank that easily breaks down
   c) equipment that is used in different areas is carrying weed spores
3 Procedures (once again, there may be more than one procedure for each cause)
   a) limit the use of support vehicles by carrying the equipment to the site
   b) select entry points that are less vulnerable
   c) clean equipment at the site before transferring it elsewhere

Monitoring

While environmental controls and procedures are critical during all construction stages, ecological sustainability does not finish once building is complete. Ongoing monitoring must be carried out in order to assess the short and long-term impacts of the enterprise. It is unlikely that all impacts, both positive and negative, have been identified — the environment is a living thing, continually moving and changing.

Ongoing monitoring includes aspects of sewage and sullage outfall, conditions of walking trails, roads and tracks, campsites, water quality, energy use, and mammal observation, tagging and monitoring.

Targets

Set realistic and time-bound targets for reducing energy and waste as well as other impacts such as land degradation and erosion. For example, aiming for a ten per cent reduction in landfill waste in the first year, is something you are likely to achieve, and so will encourage you to set more advanced targets in subsequent years.

Performance Indicators

In order to assess the level of improvement of your environment, you need to establish performance indicators. These should be easy to measure and able to provide you with the information needed. For example, most electricity and gas bills not only provide current costs and consumption but also include comparative details for the past 12 months, so you can easily track your energy use in these areas. If you are generating your own energy, regular reading of meters may be required. The state of walking tracks can be monitored by measuring the level of erosion or soil compaction in certain areas against visitor numbers, but remember that there may be other sources of track degradation, apart from visitors. If a track has been poorly sited it may erode at a high rate regardless of the number of people.

You can use visitor satisfaction as a performance indicator, particularly of your education and interpretation programs. An exit survey will reveal whether guests have understood the philosophy behind your environmental programs and energy-saving devices. This is an area often neglected by tourism operators, but educating your clients is a crucial aspect of environmental management as well as a central tenet of ecotourism. This education also has an economic aspect for your business, as once people understand why things are done in a certain way, they are more likely to accept them and enjoy their experience even more.

Responsibility for the Environment

It is important that the responsibility for environmental management goes to all levels of your organisation, and that staff are made aware of your strategy and given training where necessary. Staff accountability and involvement in the process of change will help you achieve environmental excellence as they will be working to the same ends as you. Do not assume that all your staff will naturally think the same way as you — very few will have the same commitment as the owner. However, by being involved in the audits and setting of environmental goals, they will have a greater interest and motivation in working with you.

As environmental knowledge improves, further research is undertaken and new products developed, your strategy may become out of date, so it should be reviewed annually.

Conclusion

By using many of the energy-saving, producing and waste minimisation devices outlined in this chapter, you are providing your guests and the community with visible proof of your commitment to the environment. In some cases the use of innovative technology itself has become a tourist attraction.

To maximise the benefits and reduce any problems associated with using the alternative technologies and concepts outlined in this chapter, correct environmental planning is crucial. Conducting regular environmental audits is an integral part of this planning. A qualified designer should be consulted, and various government departments and industry associations are available to help (see Appendix Three).

6 Making it Work

To be a successful tourism operator, you need to have the right product, provide good service, have strong industry networks, and plan and market your business intelligently. These points have been mentioned throughout the book, and this chapter examines them in more detail.

Starting a Tourism Business

If you are thinking about establishing any sort of tourism business, there are some points you should consider, regardless of the type of business or niche that interests you. First and foremost, tourism is a people business, so you need to assess what you have to offer from a personal point of view. Ask yourself:

- Do I like dealing with people?
  Tourism is a people business, and if you do not like dealing with people, it will be obvious, no matter how hard you try to hide it. You may also come to resent your work, which will increase stress and dissatisfaction.
- Do people enjoy my company?
  You do not have to be the life of the party, but do people tend to search you out and spend time with you, particularly at social events? The answer to this question will give you some indication of your inherent people skills.
- Do I have a sense of humour?
  A sense of humour will be appreciated by your guests and will also help you survive some of the sticky situations you are bound to encounter. A sense of humour is an excellent attribute which helps to keep things in perspective.

- Am I patient and tolerant?
  Tourists are your guests, whether they are among hundreds visiting your attraction or individuals at your B&B and you will encounter people from a wide range of cultural backgrounds.
- Am I a good organiser?
  Organisational skills are essential in tourism, as you will probably have only a small number of staff and your time will be at a premium. Good organisational skills, such as managing your time well, are a major part of running your business efficiently. If you do not have these skills, a number of training programs teach organisational techniques.
- Am I a good communicator?
  As a tourism operator you will be dealing with people from all walks of life and nationalities. Your communication skills and understanding of people are important to your operation and for dealing with other tourism businesses, suppliers and local government.
- Will I cope with disruption to normal work and home routines, and will my family cope?
  Tourists tend to be active when most people are at their leisure (hence their existence in the first place), and this is when you will be most needed — at nights, during weekends and on school holidays. You must be prepared to cope with the disruptions to yourself and your family. Also, if you have another business, such as farming, you will need to consider your busy times on the farm and see how that will (or not) fit in with peak tourism times.

If you are unsure of your answers to these questions, or you answered "no" to any of them, you should seriously reconsider your decision to become involved in tourism. However, there are some options. You may have (or decide to get) a business partner who can complement some of your weaker areas, or training may help you in the areas of organisation and communication.

Before you decide on your tourism "product", undertake some research to identify the gaps in your region so that you can create a product that is unique to the area, or at least can be differentiated from the others. Market research is examined in more detail later in this chapter.

Diversifying Your Business

Many farming families need off-farm income, particularly in times of hardship caused by drought or price fluctuations. This usually involves one or more members of the family working off the property on other farms or in local towns. These situations can create great pressure, sometimes destroying the family unit, particularly in economically and geographically peripheral regions, which often have the worst problems.

Tourism, and particularly ecotourism, can provide an alternative for some families. By running a tourism business on the property, or tours in the region, the family can remain together and survive (or even prosper!). Often a son or daughter will take on the tourism operation as their own business, which gives them an income and future they may not have had on a property unable to support the whole family.

Management

As most tourism businesses are small concerns, a tourism operator needs to be multi-skilled, doing the work of the financial planner, bookkeeper, tour guide, interpretations officer, cook and marketing manager. Many of the challenges faced by operators establishing an ecotourism business are similar to those of other small businesses and tourism operations. The major obstacles they face are under-capitalisation and under-resourcing.

An ecotourism operator must consider some extra impediments, such as the additional set-up costs associated with some minimum impact practices and increased promotional costs due to the distance from their market. Also, some operators have a relatively high public liability insurance, particularly those in a remote location or involved in conducting adventure activities. Some group insurance schemes are available through tourism industry associations that may reduce this, and if you are on the land, some farming policies can be altered to incorporate the tourism business at a minimal cost.

Some people decide to start up a tourism business because they have a hobby they want to pursue (such as bush walking, local history, hosting people) or a lifestyle they want to lead (surrounded by nature, in the peaceful countryside, a safe area for children to grow up) and they see tourism as a way to achieve these goals. This is a good starting point, but even if you are not concerned about making e a profit from your tourism business, because you have other forms of income, planning for profit is essential. No matter how much you are prepared to sacrifice for a lifestyle decision, if you are losing money on your tourism venture, in the end it will suffer.

It is important to consider doing some training in areas where you do not have experience. Local TAFE colleges offer a range of business-related courses and individual subjects, and many institutions offer courses by correspondence or "distance learning". Your local tourism association should also be able to inform you about specific tourism seminars or workshops that could help you.

Tourism is a business, and must be treated as such. Developing a business plan will help you identify where you are going and what you need and want to get from the business, including lifestyle and enjoyment.

The Business Plan

People who plan their business activities and set realistic goals are generally more successful than those who do not. Business planning is used to allocate budgets and establish cash flows, schedule your time and ensure that things are not overlooked. It is very easy, in the day-to-day pressures of running a business, to lose sight of why you are actually doing it, and a business plan will keep you on track and motivated. Also, bank and other financial institutions will not consider your request for assistance if you do not have some type of business plan that demonstrates future plans and the potential of the business.

A business plan does not have to be a massive tome, but it does follow a basic format. It will usually consist of short-term planning for the following year and a three to five year strategic plan, showing where you hope to be in that time. It should be a dynamic document that can change as situations change — it is a tool for you to use, not a rule book that you must follow to the letter. Appendix Two contains a sample business plan.

The basic structure of a business plan and the elements that should be included are:

1 The Business
   - Core Business
     One sentence that describes the main focus of your business
   - Mission Statement
     A development of your core business, including how you will achieve it ("by providing service geared to the customer's needs", or "by utilising leading environmental technology")
   - Vision
     A brief statement on how you want your business to be seen by others (either in the industry or outside)
   - Key Success Factors
     List of your attributes that will help the business to succeed
   - Business Objectives
     Generally, about three or four main business objectives should be identified, with a list of indicators that will let you know whether the objective is being achieved, along with some strategies or ways that you will go about meeting your objectives. Include a contingency plan that explains what you will do if the objective is not met. In this way you are planning for as many outcomes as you can foresee.
   - Time-lines
     Your time-line should indicate when you plan to implement your strategies as outlined previously, and over what period (say, during winter, or in the first quarter of the year).

- SWOT Analysis
  "SWOT" stands for Strengths, Weaknesses, Opportunities and Threats and is used extensively in the marketing area of a business plan. However, it is important to also include this in your overall business analysis.

  Strengths and Weaknesses refer to those areas within your business, while Opportunities and Threats relate to external influences, the "big picture". For example, one of your strengths may be that you have many native animals on your property, and a weakness may be your lack of knowledge about them — internal aspects of your business. An opportunity may be people's growing interest in native animals, and a threat may be the lack of public transport to your area — both external to your business.

  In the example in Appendix Two, "strengths" have been subdivided into "physical", "human" and "other". You may find this an easier way to focus on the specific areas.

2 The Industry
Identify the industry you are in, eg. the ecotourism industry.
- Sources of Information
  Think about and list the places where you can obtain information that may help you, and provide a good reference point.
- Associations
  Listing various industry associations that could relate to your business gives you another reference point. It also shows your bank manager that you are aware of where your business "fits in" to your industry.

3 Service and Operations Plan
- Primary Service
  This should relate to your core business as stated at the beginning of the business plan.
- Secondary Service
  This can include other services that you may be able to provide, such as catering for local functions (if you run an accommodation business).

4 Marketing Plan
This is an extremely important part of your business plan, and is often said to be the area where operators need most assistance. The next section covers marketing plans.
- Market
- Client Profile
- Competitors
- Marketing Strategy

5 Financial Information

It is important that this information is correct and presented in a way that your bank manger will understand, so contact your accountant to assist you in this area. If you decide to do it yourself, numerous short courses available at TAFE colleges and other institutions should be able to help you.

- Balance Sheets
- Projected Cash Flow
- Projected Balance Sheets and Break Even Point

6 Management

- Type of business — partnership, sole proprietor or limited liability company
- Details of proprietors and staff, including your background and any relevant information

Keep in mind that this outline and the example provided in Appendix Two are simply recommendations — you can adapt your business plan any way you like. After all, it is your business!

Networking

Chapter Three introduced the importance of developing and maintaining community networks, and just as important are tourism industry networks. As tourism is a people-oriented industry, most tourism operators are fairly social and appreciate the opportunity to meet their peers. The industry is also renowned for the helpfulness of operators towards each other — at any good tourism seminar you will find successful tourism operators running workshops on their business and advising others on how to avoid the mistakes they made.

Both official and unofficial networks would be of interest to an ecotourism operator. The official ones include tourism associations, chambers of commerce, local farming associations, Land Care committees, training centres, ecotourism associations, conservation groups, and "friends" groups. Unofficial networks can include operators and suppliers, and can be used to link ecotourism products with transport, accommodation and tours, or for cooperative booking arrangements and environmental research.

Marketing

Marketing affects everyone. It is often referred to as advertising, selling or publicity, but it is actually all of these, plus forecasting, promoting, creating, researching, analysing, planning, organising and communicating. A business that is customer-oriented, focussing on anticipating and satisfying its customer's needs and wants will have a strong marketing focus. As tourism is a people business that provides a service and experience that customers want, it needs this strong marketing focus.

Good marketing involves researching your target market, writing a marketing plan, using the media effectively and matching your product and price with people.

In tourism, a few additional marketing "rules" apply, the most important being that you should sell your area/region first, and then your product. Often your product alone will not be enough to entice people to your area, so by showing them all the other things the area has to offer you will make them want to come. Then you convince them to use your product/service.

Much has been written about marketing and many courses are available, so the marketing theory covered in this section is simply a basic introduction to the main concepts. Many tourism operators have identified the points included here as the most important and relevant ones to them.

The Five Ps

Tourism marketing is traditionally divided into five areas, that make up the "marketing mix". These are known as the "five Ps": product, price, promotion, people and place (distribution). Successful marketing integrates all these factors and recognises that they are linked.

Product

In tourism, the product is not a physical item that can be held in the hand, rather it is an intangible experience or service. A tourism product cannot actually be stored for re-sale. For example, an empty seat on an aircraft flight cannot be used after the flight has gone — it is lost forever. The product cannot be looked at and sampled prior to use. An experience can only be had once — every time will be slightly different.

To give consumers something tangible to purchase, brochures are used in lieu of the actual experience. As well as the basic information on cost and how to reach the destination, brochures should also provide some motivational items that describe the experience guests can expect. This is done through creative use of emotive words and pictures.

Price

The next chapter examines pricing in more detail, as it is closely linked with how the product is packaged in relation to other tourism products, such as transport, accommodation and tours.

Many people starting in the tourism business tend to use a "penetration" type of pricing, particularly if there are already similar products existing. Basically, penetration pricing means pricing your product below your competitors in order to gain some share of their market. As with all pricing options, this is fraught with danger and must be handled carefully to avoid a price war that you cannot support.

Promotion

Promotion covers a broad range of activities from paid advertising to public relations and brochure distribution. Paid advertising can include advertisements in local, state and national media as well as regional tourism brochures and other cooperative advertising ventures. Public relations is aimed at creating goodwill and word-of mouth promotion, and can include familiarisation tours ("famils") for travel agents, information officers and the media.

Paying for advertising, printing brochures and running famils costs money, so it is important that you know who you are targeting and how much you have to spend. Information on your target markets should be gained through your research, examined in more detail in the marketing plan below. Your budget will be established as part of your business plan.

People

As this book keeps emphasising, tourism is a people industry, dealing in providing the dreams and experiences that guests desire. Staff need to reflect the philosophy and nature of the business. This includes your family (even if they are not directly involved in the business) and any volunteer staff.

Place and Distribution

When planning your business, it is important that you consider its location. Is it near other attractions, or does it have enough to "pull" people to the area on its own? (Very few tourists businesses can achieve this). Are there other activities for people and is there accommodation (if your business is not accommodation itself!)? Also, how accessible are you, particularly in relation to public transport, the state of the roads for self-drive tourists, availability of petrol and so on?

Distribution generally relates to how you get your product sold, and the number of outlets. A wide and varied distribution is likely to attract the greatest number of people. This is closely linked with packaging and paying commissions to people to sell your product, and is covered in the next chapter.

As your brochures are the tangible evidence of your product, their distribution is linked to product distribution. They should be in visitor information centres (not just the local ones, but those "gateway" centres that feed into your region), tourist offices, travel agents (where practical) and other tourist sites. For example, a tourist attraction will carry information on places to stay, and accommodation houses will carry information on where to go and what to do.

Marketing Plan

Developing a marketing plan as part of your business plan forces you to recognise your strengths and weaknesses, your competition, and can help to identify your niche or speciality. Three basic steps are involved in developing a marketing plan:

1   Current Position

- Conduct an audit of your facilities
- Analyse your competitors
- Note any new developments in your region
- Develop a profile of your clients

2   Business Goals

Having goals for your business helps you keep focussed as you work towards them. However, they must be realistic, achievable and time-bound. For example, the goal: "to make a money" is too broad, but "to increase revenue by 10 per cent each year over the next three years" is a focussed goal that can be assessed.

3   Action Plan

The action plan provides detail on how you will achieve your goals.

The question always arises about how much money should be spent on marketing, particularly when the number of alternatives and "special offers" means it is possible to keep on spending indefinitely. A general rule of thumb is to allocate six to eight per cent of your annual turnover to marketing, however a new business or product may need to spend more while it is being established.

Research

Research is an essential tool for developing, maintaining and improving your tourism product. It is the most important area of marketing as it focuses on your customers and what they want, not what you want to do. A range of sources can be used for much of your research, so it does not have to be costly. Some of the sources that specifically handle tourism research in Australia are the Bureau of Tourism Research (BTR), state and regional tourism bodies, the Australian Tourist Commission (ATC), the Office of National Tourism (ONT), academic institutions and many industry associations. Some New Zealand sources include the New Zealand Tourism Board, Centre for Research,

Evaluation and Social Assessment (CRESA), the Foundation for Research, Science and Technology and a range of tourism conference publications, Australian, New Zealand and international. The libraries of universities with tourism programs offer a broad range of data and research publications, particularly conference proceedings and journals.

Much of the research available in relation to what ecotourists want and who they are was examined in Chapter 2, giving an overview of the broader market. However, you will need to localise your research to get a profile of visitors to your region. Your local or regional tourism association should be able to assist you with information from their own market research, or at least guide you to groups that may have more local information.

Of course, you can conduct your own research, but it can be time-consuming and costly, so it is best to use the information that is already available first. If you find you need more, local universities and colleges may be interested in assisting you as part of their studies, which would certainly save you some costs and manpower.

Personal research that is not expensive includes trying out other tourism products and surveying your own customers.

Exit Surveys

Once you are operating your tourism business, you can get customers to provide you with feedback on the product and service by asking them some simple questions when they first contact you to make a booking, and having them complete an "exit survey" after their tour, visit or stay. The type of questions that you ask may include:

- How did they hear about you?
  This provides you with feedback on your promotional activities, and indicates where you are making the greatest impression. This can (and should) be asked when they first contact you, as even if they do not actually book with you, the information is still important.
- Where are they from?
  This information will give you some indication of where you should advertise, for example in their local media or at shopping centres in the areas they have come from.
- How long did they stay?
  This will provide you with some comparative data that you can use to increase your revenue — are people staying only one night in your region? How can they be encouraged to stay two nights and increase the yield?
- Are they travelling in a family group, as a couple, singly, with friends, club or society, and what age group are they in?

These two questions will provide you with an indication of the type of people who prefer your product or region.

- What activities did they undertake?
  This is another question that will build up the profile of people who are interested in the experience you offer.
- What activities are they interested in?
  Are there additional activities that you could include in your product or that are available that they were unaware of?
- What part of their holiday is the visit to your business?
  This question is designed to find out if your business was the main reason for their visit or was something to do (or stay) on the way. If it was something on the way to another place or activity, you could consider marketing your product in conjunction with the others.

Chapter Two contains an example of a survey form, in a format that is easy for people to fill in, and allows room for extra comments. It is not always easy to encourage people to fill in your survey, particularly if they take it home with them, so try to encourage them to fill it out before they leave. Offering an incentive for them to return the survey, such as the chance to win local goods or a free trip, may also help.

Surveys and other research should be carried out over the whole lifetime of your business, as they help you keep in touch with what people want. If you are a small business and working hard to operate your enterprise, you can sometimes become so focussed on the operations side, that you don't know what is going on around you. By having your customers let you know what they think as well as where they are from, you can ascertain your progress.

Market Segmentation

In market research, market segmentation is a term used to describe groups of customers by their needs, characteristics, or behaviour. For example, Roy Morgan Research has grouped the Australian population into ten groups according to lifestyle, motivations and attitudes. These segments have been identified as:

- *Socially Aware*
  Just under ten per cent of the population, this group is aged between 35 and 49, orientated towards social issues, interested in arts and culture and are seen as wealth managers.
- *Visible Achievers*
  Just over 14.5 per cent of the population, and also aged between 35 and 49, they are success and career driven, looking for status and recognition, enjoy good family living and are the wealth creators.

- *Young Optimists*
  Aged between 18 and 24, this group makes up about seven per cent of the population. They are young and progressive, enjoy an experiential lifestyle and seeking new and different things.
- *Look at Me*
  Just over 14 per cent of the population make up this group aged between 14 and 24. They are young fun seekers, living for today, peer driven and looking for fun and freedom away from the family. They follow fashion and are extremely active.
- *Real Conservatism*
  Aged between 40 and 55, comprising five per cent of the population, they are observers of life, traditional and averse to change.
- *Something Better*
  Nine per cent of the population, aged between 25 and 34, this group consists of upwardly mobile couples who are career and lifestyle driven, but are financially stressed. Will tend to move into the Visible Achievers segment.
- *Conventional Family Life*
  Just over 11 per cent of the Australian population, this group is known as "middle Australia", aged between 30 and 49, with a strong family and home focus.
- *Traditional Family Life*
  This group also comprises slightly more than 11 per cent of the population, and is the retired "middle Australia" segment whose lives are focussed on their family. They are generally cautious of new things.
- *Fairer Deal*
  Aged between 20 and 34, this group makes up seven per cent of the population. They are generally blue collar workers and are cynical and pessimistic. They are very dissatisfied with their life.
- *Basic Needs*
  This last group is made up of widows and pensioners and comprises just over four per cent of the population. They seek protection and security as they are concerned mainly with survival.

It is generally accepted that the first four groups (Socially Aware, Visible Achievers, Young Optimists and Look at Me) are those most likely to travel and take holidays.

Other market researchers segment their markets slightly differently. The above is intended as an example of the range of market segments that can exist.

Competition

Take the time to consider who (or what) is your competition. Is it the tour operator or motel down the road, or not? Often, another operator who is offering a similar product (or experience) as you are is not your true competitor. Time and again it has been seen that when one tour operator is dong well, so are all the others — they are able to "feed" off each other and increase the profile of their region or activity.

This is particularly so with ecotourism, which accounts for about ten per cent of all nature-based experiences, increasing to 50 per cent of such experiences in areas with a recognised range of ecotourism activities and a higher number of ecotourism businesses, such as the Wet Tropics in North Queensland. Therefore, the more ecotourism-related businesses in your area, the greater the size of the market segment available to you.

Holiday activities are undertaken by people who have some disposable income, that is income left over after meeting necessities, such as food, clothing and shelter. This disposable income (or "discretionary dollar") is used to purchase luxury goods, entertainment and holidays. So your competition is any business that is trying to get hold of this discretionary income. This could include gambling, videos and even a second car. A recent advertisement for a car includes the line, "I didn't think they could afford a new car and a holiday", reflecting that often a choice must be made between two such discretionary items.

A competitor builds his business by taking away yours, so an activity such as a blockbuster show or major event in a capital city may draw people there on their annual holiday instead of to your region. The World Expo in Brisbane in 1988 brought many visitors to that city, but North Queensland destinations suffered as their traditional market chose to holiday in Brisbane instead.

Although you may not be able to compete directly with some of this competition it is important to recognise it and work with your tourism industry, rather than treating all tourism operators as your competitors.

Product Development

Through your research, you should identify the needs of your existing (or potential) customers and so develop products to match those needs. The development of your product should be ongoing, so that you are continually improving the experience offered to your customers.

It is important to perfect your product before promoting it, and research as well as a few "trial runs" should help. It is sometimes easy to forget what your tourism product really is, and end up focussing on the machinations rather than service. Your product is what your guests experience, not the seat on your bus or bed in your hostel. If your product includes tours, you could enhance the experience by providing guided tours, hosting scientific studies and expeditions, visits by schools and clubs, and other courses based on the local environment.

The name of your product is also important, as it can be a powerful markcting tool, creating images and expectations of the experience. This can also work in reverse, and an inappropriate name may raise unrealistic expectations. If you use the term "eco", your product should be ecological so that customers are not misled and the term is not devalued. Don't be one of the tourism operators who misuse the term.

Promotion

If your market does not know you exist, you will not sell your product. Promotion is the means of getting information to the market place and motivating people to purchase. It includes many advertising options — so many, in fact, that it can be difficult to decide where and how to promote your product.

Every day you will receive promotional offers, including media advertising, sponsorship opportunities, local and national trade shows, consumer travel shows, regional tourism brochure advertising, promoting on the Internet, and even CD ROM. To use your promotional funds effectively, you must be aware of your market and the sources of information it uses.

Word of Mouth

Word of mouth is the most common source of information used by ecotourists (and most other tourists as well). Unlike other products, a tourism experience cannot be replaced if it is faulty, so personal recommendations play an important role. They give other people an idea whether or not they can expect to have a pleasurable experience. So it is important to send all your customers away happy.

Articles or editorial material published in the media can assist in word of mouth promotion, as these are recognised as the writer's personal opinion, unlike a paid advertisement. Other industry personnel such as travel agents and information staff can also provide word of mouth promotion. You can get these type of recommendations by providing familiarisations ("famils") or educationals.

"Famils" and Educationals

Organised, usually free, visits to your business by travel industry staff and media may cost you some money to run but they have the potential to return that cost many times over, and this can be one of the most cost-effective forms of promotion. Famils vary in their size and complexity, from the Visiting Journalists' Program run by the Australian Tourist Commission and the New

Zealand Tourism Board for overseas journalists, through to visits by your own tourism association staff.

The media on your famil are usually visiting the whole region and will tend to write articles on it and possibly your business, whilst the travel industry staff, who include travel agents, information centre officers, helpline staff, and hotel and airport personnel can be great word-of-mouth ambassadors.

Many state and regional associations organise and coordinate famils and educationals, so it is important to keep in touch with them so that you are included. Of course, you can also organise your own visit.

TV Travel Programs

A relatively recent form of promoting tourism products are the travel programs on television. They are an excellent way of getting television coverage at virtually no cost. Like famils, the reporter and film crew experience your tourism product and talk about it on their program, providing an intimate presentation and recommendation, similar to word of mouth. Many tourism businesses are trying to appear on these programs, so you need to put some thought into your product and offer them an interesting angle on which to base their story.

Another benefit is that you may be permitted to access and use the raw footage that was filmed by the program. This, however, is up to the producers, and it may be best to approach them after the show has gone to air.

Other Media

Like the televised travel programs, travel writers and local newspapers are always looking for an interesting story. If you can provide one for them, you stand a great chance of having an article about your business printed — yet another way of utilising the power of word of mouth promotion.

You should have a media kit prepared that you can provide at any time. The information in this kit should include your brochure and business card, a one page fact sheet that provides basic information on your staff, services, location, awards you have won etc., a media release outlining an "interesting" aspect of your operation, any newsletters you produce, photocopies of articles and stories and some photos. Generally, you should provide one or two black and white photos and a colour transparency, however, it is unlikely that they will be returned to you, so only provide as much as you can afford to produce, and never give the original.

Endorsements

If you ever have a well known personality on your tour or staying with you, ask them if they will write a note saying how much they enjoyed their stay/experience and if you can use it in your promotional material. Most "famous" people would be willing to oblige if they are approached politely and made aware that you wish to quote them.

Such endorsements can add powerful support to your promotional campaign, particularly if the person is highly regarded in an area that interests your customers. A well-known naturalist or environmentalist would be an excellent endorser of an ecotourism business.

Advertising

Regardless of the type of media used for advertising, the information that you need to get across is: where you are, what your product is, what is special about it, how you can be contacted, and what it costs.

Advertising usually involves the purchase of space or time to display your message. The range of print media is extensive, and includes newspapers and magazines (general and travel-related), tourist publications, trade journals, guidebooks, telephone directories and newsletters. Print media has a long life span, and people can cut out and keep your advertisement if they wish to refer to it at a later stage, whereas television and radio are more immediate. Television is great for emotive selling, which suits tourism, but it is expensive and has a short life span. Some regional television stations can offer cheaper deals, particularly if you pool your resources with other businesses. As radio is an audio medium, it is often necessary to have a high rate of repetition to get the message across.

All forms of media should be able to provide you with information on their readers, viewers or listeners, so use this to help you make a decision. Most media will also be able to show you a demographic break-down of their audience, which will also indicate whether or not they are in your target market.

If you are interested in an offer that is being made, request a written proposal, and do not agree to anything over the phone. This will give you time to consider your options.

Brochures

Your brochure is your single most important piece of printed, as it is the tangible manifestation of the experience that you are providing. Many people will purchase your product on the strength of your brochure.

Most operators start with an all-purpose brochure, and expand into more specialised markets and products (such as other languages) later. By making the price list a separate insert, you increase the life of the brochure, as prices and tour dates are the most common areas of change.

Many decisions need to be made when designing and producing your brochure, and it is wise to collect brochures from other tourism businesses and assess their approach. Some of the main points you need to consider are:

- the size of the brochure — making them fit easily into a standard DL size envelope will reduce postage costs;
- type of paper (stock) that you use — eg recycled, thick, thin, glossy, or matt;
- whether to use full colour or not;
- whether to use photos, sketches or cartoons;
- the position of the information and pictures;
- the type of print you will use;
- the use of maps, especially "how to get there" maps.

Most brochures find their way into racks at travel agents, motels, and accommodation houses or information centres, so the paper stock should be stiff enough to stand up in the rack. Think about what part of your brochure will be visible in a brochure rack. It is usually the top quarter, so you should consider what is the most important motivational information and include it in that section.

How is your brochure going to be used, and who will use it? For example, what would your potential customer see when they open up the envelope of a posted brochure, and what do they look at first when the open it further? If the brochure is to be used by travel agents, they will be reading it upside-down as they show their customers, so they need to have vital information such as costs, dates and inclusions clearly presented so they can read them easily.

One of the most common errors in brochure design has been to include vital information (such as how to get there) on the back of the booking form, which is lost once it has been sent to confirm the booking. Once a brochure is printed it is costly and time-consuming to make further changes, so proof read it carefully, making sure that your contact details and costs are correct. Try to get a person outside your business to read it, as they will pick up details that those who are close to the operation may miss.

Distribution of the brochure is crucial, as it represents your product and is the most effective way of raising awareness and providing information in a tangible form. You should aim to have them "everywhere"! Examples of outlets for your brochure include your own premises, other attractions and facilities, visitor information centres, tourist offices, local businesses, media, seminars and conferences, your staff, related functions, train and bus terminals, travel agents, the media etc.

Professional brochure distribution companies charge a fee to keep such outlets stocked with your brochure, and can be extremely effective. They are particularly so if you are too busy running your business to visit the various outlets on a regular basis.

Also, carry brochures with you, or at least in your vehicle, wherever you go. This may sound like a basic concept, but it is surprising how many tourism operators don't do it.

Business Cards

While not as crucial as a brochure, business cards are necessary for your business dealings within the industry, and many international markets. The card should contain basic contact details with a clear and simple design. If you wish to add extra information, a folded card may suit your needs.

Marketing to Past Clients

It is substantially more expensive to gain a new client than to keep an existing one, so some effort should be expended on marketing to your past clients. This can be done simply through a follow-up thank you note or phone call, by providing special deals or rewards if they return within a specified time, or by producing a regular newsletter that is sent to your customers.

A newsletter can be a welcome reminder of the experience your customers had with you, and should contain information that will be of interest to them. For example, if you focus on a family atmosphere in your business, information on what family members and staff are doing may be relevant.

This is particularly important in the ecotourism industry as it is a quality, highly interactive type of tourism where your personality can be enhanced through direct marketing.

Guests Return to O'Reilly's

O'Reilly's Rainforest Guest House is a successful nature-based/ecotourism venture surrounded by 22,000 hectares of World Heritage listed national park in southern Queensland.

The company recognises that marketing is expensive, and that it costs much more to bring in new guests than to retain existing ones as repeat visitors. Repeat visitation at O'Reilly's is 50 to 60 per cent throughout the year, increasing to 85 per cent at Christmas.

Good customer service at the guest house is an important aspect in retaining guests, with the O'Reilly family creating an extended family atmosphere amongst themselves, guests and other staff. But what about when their guests have gone home?

The company sends more than one thousand personally written Christmas cards to their guests each year, along with a tri-annual newsletter. The newsletter provides information on what is happening in the region (both from a nature-based and tourism perspective), what the guest house is offering and some "gossip" on family and staff. According to Peter O'Reilly, it is a "newsy letter from home".

While a newsletter of this kind runs the risk of becoming another junk mail item to its recipients, the O'Reillys found that not only was it well received, but people regularly offer to pay for subscriptions, and when they include a reply paid mail response they get an excellent average response rate of 45 per cent, which is a good measure of its effectiveness.

Personal Selling

Visiting local businesses (both tourism and others), travel agents and information centres to present your product can be effective if properly organised. It is best to make appointments so that you know the people you need to speak to are available, and take along brochures, business cards and a brief video presentation if you have one.

Often the people you should be talking to are not the managers or owners of the business, but the front-line staff who are dealing with the customers — they are the ones who should be informed directly by you wherever possible.

On-Site Promotion

At your premises you have the perfect opportunity to provide guests with further promotional information. Brochure racks containing information on the region, as well as your own brochures, may encourage return visits. A wall covered with photographs of past experiences and clients creates an atmosphere of fun and reflection, or a guest book with comments from your visitors provides entertaining reading and a sense of the experience that others have also had. Scrap books containing letters from customers, newspaper articles, photos and sketches can also be extremely effective.

Consider the signage on your property, and make sure that it indicates clearly what facilities you have and where they are: from toilets or walking tracks to interpretive material, both environmental and historical.

Merchandising

Many people wish to take a memento of their experience home with them, such as photographs, videos or souvenirs. You can produce and sell your own photos and videos or just sell the film. The range of souvenirs is virtually endless, including T-shirts, caps, post cards, stickers, books, badges, stubby holders, spoons or items produced by local artisans and producers. As ecotourists are generally very socially aware, they tend to prefer locally produced items that aid the community.

It can be costly to establish a range of souvenirs, and many operators concentrate on one range such as a poster or T-shirt which may be given away as a promotional item.

Measuring Effectiveness

You need to be aware which parts of your promotional plan are the most effective and which are not. The easiest way to measure this effectiveness is by recording all the inquiries you receive and asking where they heard about you, or where they found the brochure. However, keep in mind that advertising can be useful in creating a general awareness, and whilst it might not be what prompted the person to contact you, it may have contributed.

A number of studies have been conducted to identify the sources that people use to find out about tourism products. In one of these studies the Bureau of Tourism Research looked at where international tourists go to find out about nature based activities. The results are shown in the table below.

	Newspaper/ Magazine articles (%)	Travel Agent(%)	Advertisements in Newspaper/Magazine (%)	Other(%)
United States	25.2	13.6	4.8	56.3
Canada	37.1	0.5	12.0	50.5
UK & Ireland	17.5	4.3	4.3	73.4
Germany	20.9	20.8	5.7	51.9
Scandinavia	18.0	6.1	9.1	64.1
Other Europe	18.4	15.1	2.7	62.5
Japan	6.8	50.8	1.3	41.1
Other Asia	14.7	30.7	5.2	49.4
Other Countries	12.9	18.4	13.5	55.2
Total	18.0	19.6	5.3	56.6

Source: BTR International Visitors Survey, 1994

Although the above survey does not cover all forms of advertising, as indicated by the high percentages in the "other" category, it gives some indication of the preferred sources for various international markets. For example, many western countries use travel agents less than Asian countries, and all countries use newspaper articles more than actual advertisements. The influence of articles compared with advertisements is important, as many people feel that they are getting a less biased view from a travel writer (who most likely went on a famil).

Cooperative Marketing

The costs of marketing an individual tourism product, particularly in a niche area like ecotourism, can be very high, especially as you will probably need to promote your region as well. However, these costs can be made more realistic through marketing cooperatively with other tourism and related businesses, enabling you to market your product more extensively. If you can identify common themes or interests with the community as well as across regions, and promote neighbouring attractions, mutual benefits will follow.

As well as reducing the cost of your marketing, you may find that by working in with others you actually broaden the market you are reaching and by associating yourself with "good" products and concepts you enhance your own company's image. Of course, you will need to consider the consequences of teaming up cooperatively so that such association does not work to your detriment.

Local, regional, and state tourism bodies offer many cooperative marketing opportunities, often providing advertising in their publications. Also, many tourism associations and groups offer the opportunity to be represented at trade shows. The Australian Tourist Commission offers cooperative advertising programs into the international market.

Industry associations such as the Ecotourism Association of Australia may provide the opportunity to market cooperatively with like-minded tourist businesses through networking and other initiatives.

You may find that advertising and promoting your business in conjunction with other businesses in your area is not only cost-effective, but also expands your market. They do not have to be tourism businesses, but you may find a strong connection between your tourism product and other local businesses that can be used to benefit you all.

International Marketing

The international market is an important one for ecotourism, as overseas visitors have a higher participation rate in environmental tourism than any other forms. However, it is important that you get your product right in the domestic market before actively engaging in international marketing, as it is a big step. It can take up to five years of continual promotion before any real returns are seen, so you must be able to operate your business with the domestic market in the mean time. Many tourism businesses regard international tourists as icing on the cake, making up 10 to 20 per cent of their business. Some groups can also be extremely fickle as their travelling experience increases, looking for new destinations and experiences.

It is likely that you will get some international guests, usually travelling as FITs (Fully Independent Travellers) who come with local friends or locate your business through your domestic marketing program. Use these visitors to research the potential of the international market by finding out as much as you can about them and keeping in touch with them after they leave. Their reactions will give you some idea of which international markets may be interested in your product.

Each international market has its own distinct characteristics, but most of them have a number of common perceptions of Australia and New Zealand — lands of natural wonders, the "final frontier" with vast spaces and strange animals, and high quality service and accommodation. However, Australia and New Zealand are also seen as expensive locations, due to their distance from many countries.

Australia and New Zealand is a dream destination for many, and ranks very highly in terms of desirability, often being the most desired destination to visit in the world. This is not only because of the images mentioned above, but also a perception that the region is safe to visit with friendly, relaxed people and a cultured lifestyle.

Size of the Inbound Nature Tourism Market

According to figures obtained from the International Visitors Survey (IVS), 1994, by the Bureau of Tourism Research, more than half the international tourists visited a national park, a quarter taking part in a bushwalk or rainforest walk, 12 per cent coral viewing, eight per cent visiting Aboriginal sites and two per cent taking an outback safari. Some of these percentages may not seem very high, but remember, we are talking about 3.1 million international tourists for 1994. So, 248,000 visited an Aboriginal site and 62,000 went on an outback safari. The growth of the inbound tourism market is expected to continue at a steady rate, and contribute significantly to increased employment and new businesses in the tourism industry.

However, of the tourists interviewed for the IVS, only five per cent said that experiencing outdoor, nature-based activities was a particular influence on their decision to travel to the region. This indicates that the number of dedicated ecotourists visiting Australia and New Zealand is small, and that most international tourists come to this region for a variety of reasons and undertake a variety of activities. Many of the "purist" international ecotourists tend to travel in third world countries.

So, when marketing an ecotourism product overseas, it is important to reach a broad range of potential travellers, rather than focus specifically on ecotourists. Of course, if more ecotourists were aware of the development of ecotourism in Australia and New Zealand, they may decide to come here instead of South America.

The table on page … showed that newspaper and magazine articles rated highly, along with travel agents in certain countries, as sources of information for nature based tourists. Travel books and guides are also a major source of influence on the international traveller. If you are planning to promote your business internationally, you will need to look at such information carefully and plan how to gain the maximum effective coverage.

Trade Shows

The Australian Tourist Commission promotes Australia overseas to 174 countries. It is an excellent source of information on international markets and provides many cooperative marketing opportunities as does the New Zealand Tourism Board. The opportunities (besides media advertising) include participation in trade shows such as Aussie Trading Post, the Australian Tourism Exchange, Japan Australia Mission (JAM), International Tourism Bourse (ITB) etc., as well as the Visiting Journalists Program and other famils. State tourism bodies are also involved in many of these areas and have international representatives in many of their major overseas markets.

While most international tourism trade shows are held overseas, the Australian Tourism Exchange (ATE) is held in Australia annually. Overseas buyers (wholesalers) travel to the show to familiarise themselves with Australian inbound tourism products, and often make decisions as to whether or not to include them in their programs and packages. Each operator has a 15 minute interview session with a buyer where they have the opportunity to present their tourism product on an individual level. This can be daunting for entrants into international tourism, but there are alternatives for those starting out, and there is always the option of sharing a booth.

In Victoria, a Group Tourism Exchange is also run annually to showcase tourism products that may be suitable for the group travel market. It is run in a similar way to the ATE. Inbound tour operators and social and sporting organisations are usually very interested in this area. You should be able to find other programs run by other states and some even regionally.

Points to Remember

A number of points need to be kept in mind when dealing with the international market. Many of them may seem obvious, but they are still worth noting. By putting yourself in the position of a foreign tourist, many of these points should make sense.

Your credibility in the industry is extremely important, as most people will not be prepared to travel, visit or stay with an operator who has little experience — another reason for getting your product right in the domestic market first. You may also need to re-think your target markets, as you may find that certain groups in some countries will enjoy your product most — just as with the Australian market. A separate marketing plan may be needed for the international market.

An important issue for international travellers is your location, particularly in relation to access and transport. Few overseas visitors will have their own transport, so they must be able to reach you through the public transport system, private services or via a tour. They often have an unrealistic image of the distances in Australia, so be aware of their lack of understanding in this area.

International tourists poring over their travel agent's range of tourist brochures will look for a recognisable regional image, name or logo that readily identifies the country. In your promotional material, it is important that you include the word "Australia" and/or "New Zealand" in a prominent position, and use the ATC's Australian logo (if relevant) which can be obtained from them. Also, if you are translating your brochure into another language, make sure it is professionally done.

Finally, be aware of overseas postage costs, as you can soon become severely out of pocket with excessive postage bills. For example, sending 50 packets of information to the United States may cost at least $75! It may be worth considering other forms of disseminating information such as the Internet and email.

Environmental Policy as a Marketing Tool

In Chapter 5 we looked briefly at developing an environmental plan. Central to this plan is a policy that you and your staff are committed to following. This policy can be effectively used as a powerful marketing tool, particularly in relation to ecotourism.

The very nature of an ecotourism business suggests that the company is conscious of the environment and the impact that tourism can have. By producing a simple environmental policy based on your environmental plan, that can be promoted to your staff and clients, they will become educated in your philosophy. You could develop a "policy statement" and display it on your premises and in your promotional literature. Such a statement could include your position on:

- waste management and recycling
- energy conservation
- water conservation
- minimum impact tourism
- education and research
- conservation support
- community support
- purchasing policies
- landscaping

and so on....

While most ecotourists are well-educated and conservation aware, they may still need the measures you are undertaking explained to them, and may want to learn more. A policy statement or code of practice shows them the range and scope of environmental issues that the company is addressing. Using comparisons can highlight improvements, such as stating that "our recycling of glass and metal is up five tonnes from last year", or "the energy cost per guest per night has been reduced by 25 per cent since introducing solar power".

If you train your staff to explain these issues to your guests, not only will the guests appreciate it, but the staff will also find increased pride in their environment, and work harder to keep it that way.

Environmental information also can be used in promotional material and as a basis for articles or stories in many publications, both locally and overseas.

Emphasising Environmental Commitment

Fiordland Ecology Holidays in New Zealand has developed a Code of Ethics that it uses in its promotional material as confirmation of the company's environmental commitments:

Our Code of Ethics

- Lowest possible impact on the environment
- Guaranteed personal attention
- To support research through tourism
- Treat all life forms with love and respect

Research projects we have helped fund through tourism include, weevils, skinks, dolphins, seals, marine research, whales, albatross, predator eradication, re-forestation and work with New Zealand native birds.

A Final Note on Marketing...

You should market your tourism product to your own staff, family members and local community as well as to your customers!

Codes of Practice and Accreditation

Codes of Practice recommend and reinforce ethical behaviour in many industries and are common in ecotourism. Many professional associations have a code of practice or code of ethics that they require their members to follow. These codes usually cover areas of appropriate behaviour between the operator and their clients as well as between each other and behaviour towards the natural environment.

Most of the codes of practice are voluntary as they are not enforceable through law. Many industries realise that if they do not undertake some form of self-regulation, the government may step in and establish legally binding regulations that may be extreme, or carry extremely high penalties for non-compliance.

While codes of practice are not legally enforceable, they can be controlled to a certain extent through membership of professional associations. For example, house builders must abide by the code of practice that has been established by the Australian Housing Association, in order to belong to that association. So, even though some of the requirements in the code may not be legal requirements, by breaking them, they risk losing their membership of the association.

The tourism industry has many associations with codes of practice that their members must abide by, including the following environmentally-based ones:

- IAATO Environmental Protocol (International Association of Antarctic Tour Operators)
- ATIA Code of Environmental Practice (now known as Tourism Council Australia (TCA))
- EAA Code of Practice (Ecotourism Association of Australia)
- Northern Territory Tourist Commission Code of Practice
- PATA Code for Environmentally Responsible Tourism (Pacific Asia Travel Association)

A number of codes have also been developed for specific activities, whether they are run by tourism operators or private individuals. They include:

- National Parks Horse Riding Code
- Minimal Impact Bushwalking Code (Australian Alps National Parks)
- Car-based Camping Code (Australian Alps National Parks)
- Mountain Bike Code (Australian Alps National Parks)
- IAATO Guidance for Visitors to the Antarctic

These activity-specific codes often form part of the Codes of Practice of the industry associations, for example, all horseback tour operators must abide by the National Parks Horse Riding Code if they wish to be members of the Australian Tourism Operators Association. Your local regional tourism association should be able to inform you of any codes of practice or ethics that tourism businesses in your area are required to meet.

It is now recognised that merely agreeing to abide by a code of practice is not enough, and many industry sectors have sought to obtain stronger compliance, particularly in relation to the environment. This is where "accreditation" comes in.

Ecotourism Accreditation

Accreditation can benefit both the visitor and tour operator by providing a quality tourism experience, training opportunities, recognition, and by giving a marketing identity and edge to the product. Ecotourism accreditation also benefits natural areas and the land management agencies through increasing appropriate environmental behaviour and encouraging responsibility for the management of the environment.

In late 1996, after years of industry consultation, the Ecotourism Association of Australia (EAA) and Australian Tourism Operators Association (ATOA) launched a detailed accreditation program for ecotourism operators, known as the National Ecotourism Accreditation Program (NEAP).

According to the EAA, the program is based on the following eight principles:

1 Ecotourism focuses on personally experiencing natural areas in ways that lead to greater understanding and appreciation;

2 Ecotourism integrates opportunities to understand nature areas into each experience;

3 Ecotourism represents best practice for ecologically sustainable tourism;

4 Ecotourism productively contributes to the conservation of natural areas;

5 Ecotourism provides constructive ongoing contributions to local communities;

6 Ecotourism is sensitive to, interprets, and involves different culture, particularly indigenous culture;

7 Ecotourism consistently meets clients' expectations;

8 Ecotourism marketing is accurate and leads to realistic expectations.

Each of these principles is reflected in specific assessment criteria that establish two levels of accreditation, namely core and advanced.

The accreditation process is similar to other established industry programs, where applicants assess the performance of their own business against the criteria and qualify their answers with a brief explanation and any relevant supporting material. A random audit will also be conducted of about 10 per cent of accredited businesses annually, as well as feedback from clients.

The Federal Government supports the program, and in future, some promotional opportunities will only be available to accredited tourism operators, be they in ecotourism or other areas.

Further information can be obtained from the EAA or ATOA (see Appendix Three).

Risk Management

As most ecotourism operations are in the outdoors, and many incorporate adventure activities in their program, the probability of accidents is very real. An integral part of any accreditation program (and any business) is the establishment of procedures to minimise risk and limit the damage of any accidents that may occur. Too often risk management procedures are only implemented after a serious accident, rather than as part of the overall business planning strategy.

The example below provides an extreme case:

Drawing up lists of every conceivable accident, its possible causes (people-related, staff, equipment, climatic conditions) and ways to minimise its potential and severity will help you and your staff handle many difficult situations.

Regular safety inspection of all your equipment, vehicles and facilities must be undertaken, as well as planning what to do in the case of an accident or emergency. It is all very well to be qualified in first aid, but if the first aid kit is not up to standard or you (or your staff) have forgotten how to use the communication equipment, your initial investment in training has been useless.

Tragedy Leads to Management Changes

In April 1995 at Cave Creek in New Zealand, 14 people were killed when the viewing platform they were standing on collapsed. The platform had been poorly constructed by well-meaning but unqualified staff, and did not meet building standards.

Soon after Cave Creek, more than 60 structures were closed pending upgrade or removal, with more being added to the list as the Department conducted an inventory of the thousands of structures for which it was responsible.

As a result of this tragedy, the managing agent, the Department of Conservation, developed a quality management system for use in all aspects of its operations. The system has four main elements that will be incorporated into every task the Department undertakes:

1 Objectives
2 Accountabilities
3 Procedures
4 Standards

The quality management system has provided a new way of thinking about the management of visitor structures, and accountability has led managers to ensure the safety of the structures for which they are responsible. This has necessitated a strategic systems approach to the construction and maintenance of park facilities.

Conclusion

Once the initial excitement over the great idea has died down, and before your business begins, you should implement a range of processes. These include deciding if you are truly suited to the industry, through to ascertaining if your other sources of income can work in a complementary manner with the tourism venture.

A business plan is absolutely essential, and financial institutions require it before they will consider any financing application. The plan is important because it requires you to focus on your idea and bring it from your imagination into the real world. The development of a marketing strategy is also important, with the "Five Ps", of product, price, promotion, people and place/distribution forming the basis of the plan. And do not forget your past clients when promoting your product.

Research needs to be carried out during the conceptual and planning stages of the business, but it is also important to continue to research and monitor customer satisfaction as well as to be aware of overall industry trends. Much information in this area is available from government organisations.

Adherence to a code of practice and/or industry accreditation are extremely important for ecotourism operators, as the basis of your product is protection (or minimal impact) of the environment. By adhering to codes and obtaining accreditation you not only protect your business for the future, but also possess a powerful promotional advantage over other tourism businesses.

7 Making it Pay

Some tourism operators become involved in the industry, not to make money, but for lifestyle or ethical reasons. Tourism enables them to maintain a rural living, with product decisions based on personal preferences rather than economics. However, without an eye on "the bottom line", even those with the highest ideals will fail. Profit margins for the small operator are tight and the industry can be fragmented due to the intensity of the work and remoteness of operators. Also, the per capita expenses of many nature based tours (particularly ecotourism) are larger than high-volume tourism due to the small group sizes, remoteness, additional equipment and transportation, need for an expert or specialist guide and the cost of contributing towards maintenance of the resource.

This chapter briefly covers the principles of pricing and distribution as well as some of the main legal considerations relevant to ecotourism and tourism in general.

Any tourism business must be profitable, able to pay commissions and yet still be considered by the consumer as value-for-money. If any of these elements are out of balance, the business will suffer. Many tourism products in Australia and New Zealand are underpriced, with their profit margins set below feasible levels. This affects their long-term viability, but operators are afraid to challenge the market by pricing their product above their competitors, to the detriment of themselves and the industry. All costs, including personal living expenses must be considered in order to sustain your business in the long term.

The areas that need to be considered include basic costs, desired return, competitors' prices, what the market will bear, commissions to agents and the position of your product in the market place. Where many small tourism businesses come unstuck is structuring their pricing to incorporate commissions, and we will look at this aspect after the distribution chain is examined.

Distribution
Domestic

It is not practical to actively sell your product and run it at the same time, relying on customers to contact you directly. For this reason, most tourism products are also sold through agents. For the domestic tourism market, the distribution chain is relatively simple, with the customer booking either directly with the operator, or using a retail travel agent or other simple product distributor such as a tourist information centre or booking agent. These agents can be licensed travel agents or booking services who on-sell to the general public, as well as wholesalers who group products into packages for sale by agents.

International

Distributing your product to the international market is a little more complex than selling it to domestic travellers. The end customer makes their booking through a retail travel agent in their own country, who has sourced your product via an inbound tour operator based in Australia/New Zealand, who in turn has obtained your product either directly from you or through a tour wholesaler.

For example, if you are selling your tours to Germany, a wholesale agent may incorporate it into a package tour, pass it on to the inbound operator who has business arrangements with travel agents in Germany, who then sell the entire package to their customers. (A tour wholesaler can be either in your country or based overseas.)

Working with an Inbound Tour Operator

The inbound tour operator (ITO) is your link with the international marketplace. An inbound operator can take your product into areas that you may not have access to (due to the high cost of promoting a single product), or even be aware of, such as new and emerging international markets. Also, as inbound operators only deal in the international market, they are specialists and have a cultural understanding of doing business in those markets — a distinct advantage in dealing with other nationalities.

Benefits of using an inbound operator include:

- experience and knowledge
- extension of your business's marketing arm
- ability to market and see the total product
- easy access to booking offices for yourself and your international clients as the ITO can often be contacted outside standard business hours

- lower communication costs as the ITO handles all the international communications
- centralised billing and accounting with the ITO paying you, not the overseas agent
- cultural experience in selected markets

The Inbound Tourism Organisation of Australia (ITOA) and the Inbound Tour Operators Council of New Zealand (ITOC) have directories of all licensed inbound operators in their respective countries and can advise on the selection of an inbound operator that will suit your needs, such as those specialising in nature-based and ecotourism. Appendix Three contains contact details.

However, about 60 per cent of international tourists arrive without making any bookings, so you need to maintain your local distribution channels with domestic travel agents, state tourism bodies and visitor information centres.

Booking Sources

Bookings come from many sources, including those mentioned above. The list includes:

- retail travel agents, domestic and international
- centralised booking services
- government travel centres
- motoring associations
- visitor information centres
- tour wholesalers
- computer reservation systems (used by agents)
- the Internet (can be used by everyone)
- bookings made direct to the tourism business

Often your local visitor information centre will coordinate bookings, coach tours, lunches and visits to attractions on behalf of inbound tour operators, so it is important that the staff at the centre are familiar with your product.

A number of different arrangements are possible with agents. For example, you may want them to contact you personally before confirming a booking so that you maintain control over visitor numbers. However, if you are running a tourism business, be it accommodation, attraction or tour, you will not always be available to respond to their requests immediately (particularly with overseas agents). Most of the time, the agent will have their customer with them, and require a response as soon as possible. If they are not able to contact you they will probably go elsewhere.

Another option is to provide them with a specified number of beds per night or spaces on your tour that they can sell without getting confirmation from you. They are usually permitted to sell them only up to a certain date, such as one month before the tour/accommodation. After that, any unsold spaces are returned to you to either sell direct or through them with your approval. While many agents prefer this arrangement, you must decide who you will provide with this facility, and how long they are able to hold their option.

The Internet is an information source that can also be used as a direct booking system. Millions of people around the world have access to the "Net" and the World Wide Web. So far, most people use the Internet to obtain information and still book through travel agents. However, it offers great potential for niche industries such as ecotourism to access the international marketplace. Green travel groups and industry associations have pages on the Internet, as well as government tourism associations; and you can produce your own page at a reasonable cost. The Australian Tourist Commission and New Zealand Tourism Board have a range of services and information on accessing and utilising the Internet. Also, as security improves, more people will be prepared to book and pay via the Internet.

The growth of computer reservation systems can solve many of the problems relating to booking and distribution, by providing direct access to your own data, confirming the availability of beds, seats, or places immediately without having to make personal contact. Such computerised systems will benefit all businesses, particularly those in remote areas (such as many ecotourism operators). Of course, there are costs involved in establishing such systems, but these can be limited by cooperating with other businesses and forming distribution and booking networks for ecotourism products.

Distribution and Booking Networks

Tourism operators agreeing to pool their resources and work together (as well as structured, commercial enterprises) have established cooperative networks. A non-tourism example of this approach is the Ticketmaster ticketing service, that promotes and sells tickets to various events on commission.

Cooperative Booking Service

The Host Farms Association in most states of Australia offers a free booking service to the general public. This is a cooperative venture between the members of the Association, and is a cost-effective way for the many host farms to handle their bookings. The booking service is available during business hours — times when you are not always personally available on your property — to give potential customers a reliable information and reservation service.

By belonging to your relevant industry association, such cooperative ventures can be undertaken at a minimal cost to your business (usually on commission).

Commissions

All the agents, wholesalers and inbound operators who promote and market your product on your behalf are paid only when they actually make a booking — they are paid on results, that is, commission. When considering your pricing, even if you do not intend to sell to international tourists, you must factor in these commission payments. It is not advisable to add them on to your price after it has been set. It is also unethical to have a separate price for international tourists unless they are being offered a different product than the local market.

Commissions will comprise at least 30 per cent of your price, with 10 per cent going to the retail agent, 10 to 15 per cent to the wholesaler and a further 10 to 15 per cent to the inbound operator. Although this may sound high, remember that they are promoting your product and are only paid on results — if they do not sell it, you do not pay.

You can limit the number of spaces you sell on commission, or block out times of the week/year that they are unable to book, particularly if you have a "high season" that you are currently filling through direct sales. So, spaces booked from commissioned agents are often those that would have been empty — they are a bonus.

Packaging

"Packaging" usually refers to the wrapping around a physical product, but in tourism it relates to bringing a range of items (tourism products) together and tying them in to a package. By combining these items, a more attractive, integrated and larger product can be offered. Hence the term, "package tour", which has connotations of mass tourism. However, even small, niche tourism products such as ecotourism can be packaged in a manner that will benefit both the operators and their customers.

For example, combining transport and accommodation with your walking tour will enable people to easily travel to your area and stay there, as well as taking the tour. Not only do you benefit from the attraction of providing additional services, but so do the other businesses. This can also work the other way, with people considering staying in an area deciding to take the package that includes your tour with their preferred accommodation.

Such added value is particularly appealing to international tourists without their own transport and with little knowledge of the area they are visiting. However, domestic tourists are also interested in packages. The challenge for many ecotourism operators is to ensure that the package does not appear to be a mass tourism product, as most nature-based tourists consider themselves to be independent travellers and avoid large tours. Small, specialist packages and tours are recommended.

An Ecotourism Package

One wholesaler with a retail travel agency "shop-front" is Kiwi Eco Adventures. By combining a number of individual ecotourism products into a range of flexible packages, the agency can offer a high profile product and afford to promote it extensively. The following is an extract from the company's Internet site:

Kiwi Eco Adventures Ltd (KEA) is a boutique travel agency offering the personalised touch for travellers who want to be independent and experience some of the most thrilling and awe-inspiring eco-adventure activities on offer in New Zealand's unspoilt natural environments.

KEA has something for everyone. If you seek adventure we can offer you New Zealand's best in sea kayaking, hiking, climbing and more. With KEA you can get the adrenaline flowing on white water rafting trips through sheer gorges and bush clad cliffs, or feel the magic of an abseiling and rafting journey into silent underworld cave systems.

For those more sedate travellers there is the internationally renowned adventure of whale watching, or guided tours into the enthralling habitats of New Zealand's native bird species, including the endangered little flightless feathered kiwi.

We have selected the finest scenic boat cruises and short scenic flights and you can experience the culture, songs and dance of New Zealand's indigenous Maori in traditional tribal settings.

You simply tell us what you want to do from the wide range of activities offered here, and we'll coordinate them with transport and accommodation for the time you have available.

The main advantages of pre-booking with KEA are to save you precious time in planning your holiday and minimise missing out on popular adventures due to over-booking.

The adventure activities (guided and unguided) are run by experienced and hand-picked tour operators. If you don't want a total itinerary we can just book the activities, accommodation or just the transport.

KEA provides sample itineraries containing what we believe is the best each region has to offer. These can be linked together for longer holidays or amended to suit your party's specific desires. With each regional sample we list alternative activities that you may want to include or substitute into the itinerary.

Quality accommodation, bed and breakfast style, and transport, hand-picked like the tour operators, is all part of the KEA package.

KEA has also listed several national tour operators who can organise a New Zealand trip focused entirely on one activity, for example, hiking in New Zealand's national parks, mountainbiking, and geological and wildlife tours.

Some Broad Legal Considerations

Many laws relating to tourism are aimed at protecting the customer and the operator. This section is planned to provide you with a basic overview of the legislation that particularly affects tourism businesses, including the EC Directive.

Consumer Protection

Consumer protection legislation in Australia includes the Trade Practices Act 1974 (Federal) and the Fair Trading Act (State). The Fair Trading Acts differ between each state, but they cover all the relevant sections of the Trade Practices Act, so it is possible to consider the federal Act to gain an understanding of the legal requirements regarding consumer protection. In New Zealand, protection is in the Fair Trading Act 1986 and has similar provision to the Trade Practices Act.

The sections in the Trade Practices Act that relate to tourism are service-oriented and include:

Section 52   *Misleading or deceptive conduct*
This Section has been designed to "catch" any conduct that is not covered by the following Sections, and as such is very broad.

Section 53   *False or misleading representation (incorrect statements)*
This deals with specific false or misleading statements in connection with the supply of services.

For example, a country-based tour operator leads you to believe that they will collect you personally from the local train station; instead, someone else collects you in a beat-up vehicle that is smelly and uncomfortable. The operator could be held liable if this misleading information caused you to enjoy your tour less than you would have if they had collected you personally, as you had understood.

Section 55A   *Certain misleading or deceptive conduct in relation to services*
This deals with kinds of conduct that may mislead the public in relation to the services provided by the business or trader.

For example, an exclusive guest house providing "unique and special" accommodation that has an expensive looking exterior and well-presented staff may lead you to believe that the rooms will be of a similar standard. If they are not, the operator may be liable.

Section 58   *Acceptance of payment without intending to supply as ordered*
This deals with companies giving services that are significantly different from those promised when paid for.

For example, you pay for a luxury holiday in a five-star resort, but when you get there renovations are being done and many of the services you paid for (and expected), such as the pool, water slide, and gymnasium, are not available. The agent who booked the trip and the business that accepted the reservation could be held liable under Section 58.

Section 74 *Sellers' duty in relation to supply of services*
This Section requires that the business conducts itself with due care and skill.

Generally speaking, this legislation means that there must be no misleading impressions given about the price and quality of services, and the consumer must be told of any variations to a product as soon as possible.

Travel Advertising Guidelines (TAG)

The Trade Practices Commission administers the Trade Practices Act and has also issued a range of Travel Advertising Guidelines that are controlled under the Act. These guidelines, which are referred to as TAG 1, 2, ...etc. were designed, not to prohibit imaginative advertising, but to ensure that the use of advertising devices is acceptable and not misleading or deceptive. The distinction is sometimes very fine.

TAG 3 outlines the main areas of concern and how the Trade Practices Commission plans to administer the application of the Act:

"There are two broad areas of conduct in the travel industry which give rise to concern:

(a) representations in promotional literature that create misleading impressions of the price at which services are offered, the quality or range of services offered or the time at which services are to be provided and their duration; and

(b) failure to inform consumers of variations to price, quality, itineraries or the like upon which claims in promotional literature material to a consumer's decision to travel are based."

The areas that the TAGs cover include:

- *Notice of variations*
  A consumer who has committed to a travel service (usually by paying a deposit) should be given adequate notice of any variation as to price, quality or itinerary of the promoted services. The consumer must be notified at the first possible moment.

- *Representations of price*
  There should be no misunderstanding about the price of a service. As advertised, it should be informative and made clear whether it is all inclusive or only a basic price to which additional charges may be added.

  For example, many tours provide breakfast, but not other meals within the cost; or optional tours may be offered. The consumer must be made aware of the cost of these additional expenses.

- *Representations about services*
Promotional material must not exaggerate the quality or extent of services offered to such a degree that the services advertised are materially different from what is actually available.

  For example, advertising "bungalows with all modern conveniences in a tropical rainforest", if the showers do not have hot water and the toilet system is a "drop style" (not flushing), could be found to be in breach of the TAGs. This is particularly relevant to ecotourism operations who provide services that are may be unfamiliar to some people, such as composting, non-flushing toilets and recycling mechanisms. You do not have to detail every service you provide, just be clear about what (and how) you promote.

- *Representations about the duration of the tour, holiday or time of travel*
In describing the duration of a tour, holiday or travel, the customer must be given as clear an idea as possible of the length of time of the tour and the time spent at any stopovers.

  For example, a tour that arrives at Uluru at 6.30 pm on the first day and departs at 7.00 am on the fourth day should be described as "three days, four nights Uluru" rather than "four days Uluru".

- *Representations about finance*
"Fly Now – Pay Later", or any other statements about finance should be written in terms that will not mislead the "average person" — a term used in many legal circumstances (much time is often spent in the courts debating what an "average person" is).

- *Bait advertising*
Some irresponsible tourism operators advertise a holiday, tour, accommodation or transportation at a super special price without ever intending to offer the product. This is known as "bait advertising", and is used to attract customers, who are then sold a more expensive tour or holiday. It is regarded as a deceptive practice.

  An advertisement should be very clear as to the number of tickets or places available at the "special price" in order to avoid a charge of misleading advertising.

- *Over bookings*
Many operators over-book due to the incidence of "no-shows", however if you do this, you are under an obligation to honour all bookings. There are many examples where people have not been able to obtain a seat on a flight, a room in a hotel or place on a tour for which they thought they had firm reservations. Such conduct could be seen as misleading or deceptive and contravene the Trade Practices Act.

However, some matters are considered to be outside an individual's or company's control, including government approved fare increases, exchange rate fluctuations, strikes, warfare or natural disasters. Promotional material should state that these matters may affect their services, usually in the booking section of a brochure, in the "fine print" under terms and conditions.

Use of Confidential Information

Many people in the tourism industry move from company to company, often taking information from their previous employer, particularly information about customers and suppliers, to their new job. As the number of employees signing workplace agreements and employment contracts increases, many are being asked to agree to a clause which prohibits them from taking or using documents or information after they leave the business.

Employees can be restrained from taking any paperwork or copies of papers (especially lists of customers, and even diaries) with them when they leave, as these items remain the property of the employer who can recover them by legal action. However, an employer cannot stop an employee from taking away any skills, knowledge or education acquired while working for the business.

Confidential information or ideas can be protected under the laws of copyright.

Copyright Protection

Another area that is relevant to tourism is that of copyright — the protection of the expression of an idea (it cannot exist in an idea alone). The idea can be expressed in many ways — the laws of copyright protect most of the literary, musical, dramatic and artistic work produced in Australia and New Zealand.

Travel brochures and tour itineraries are considered (from the point of view of the law!) as literary works, and are therefore covered by copyright. If you copy great chunks from a tour brochure and include it in your own with no changes, you could be sued for breach of copyright. However, with a few changes, you will usually be safe.

A good example of this is shown in the case study in the Box. Although it is not directly related to tourism, it is clear and set a precedent for following cases. This shows that the level of originality does not have to be great, but just has to appear different when published.

Logos, drawings and photographs published in a travel brochure are all considered to be artistic works, so do not print a photograph without the permission of its owner. For example, if one of your past clients sent you some photos of the trip they enjoyed so much, you need to get their permission to reproduce them.

Legal Case Study

John Fairfax and Sons Pty Ltd v Consolidated Press Ltd (1960)

The Daily Telegraph published birth and death notices that it took from earlier editions of the Sydney Morning Herald. A few changes were made in the Daily Telegraph's notices, such as abbreviating dates, omitting the letters "RIP" and altering some adjectives such as "dearly departed". The Sydney Morning Herald sought to stop these notices appearing in the Daily Telegraph, claiming breach of copyright.

The Supreme Court of New South Wales held that the Sydney Morning Herald had copyright over the way they appeared in the newspaper, not over the original announcements. The notices in the Daily Telegraph were found to be sufficiently altered so that they had now become original works in their own right.

Source: Cordato, A, "Australian Travel and Tourism Law"

Copyright on literary and artistic works lasts for the life of the creator plus a further 50 years from the author's death. For photographs, the copyright lasts for 50 years from when it was first published, which actually means from when the negative was developed. It cannot be extended.

If one of your staff writes a brochure for your operation, who owns the copyright? If it has been produced in the course of their employment or under a specific contract, you (the employer) are the initial owner of the copyright.

So, be aware of the copyright regulations, particularly when preparing promotional material, and if in doubt obtain legal advice as it can be a complex area.

Contracts

Legally speaking, a contract is an oral, written, or implied set of promises. Of course, it can be very difficult to prove that something was said or implied if there are no independent witnesses, so a written contract is the easiest to prove.

Requirements of a Contract — Offer and Acceptance

In order for a contract to exist, there must be a definite offer, acceptance of that offer and consideration provided. In legal terms, consideration is the conferring of a benefit (usually money) from one party on the other.

In its simplest form, a contract comes into existence on acceptance of an offer. "Acceptance" can be in the form of handing money over (consideration) and being given a ticket to travel, such as a train or tram ticket.

Terms of the Contract

As mentioned earlier, terms (like promises) can be in writing, by word of mouth (oral statements) or implied. If a major promise is broken, the injured party may end the contract; if a minor promise is broken, the contract may still remain, but compensation would be payable.

To be legally entitled to enter into a contract, both parties must be over 18 years old, sane, and must have legal identities (this can be a person or a registered company, but not just a business name, which is not a legal identity). A bankrupt person (or insolvent company) is not permitted to enter into a contract.

If a person has been encouraged into making a contract by false statements or unfair or harsh conduct, the contract is not legally binding.

Legal Case Study

The Balmain New Ferry Co Ltd v Robertson (1906)

The Balmain Ferry Company conducted a ferry service in Sydney from Circular Quay to Balmain. To travel from Circular Quay, the intending passenger paid a penny to pass though a turnstile onto the wharf area and board the ferry. There was no turnstile at the Balmain end, and the passenger did not have to pay to leave or enter the wharf. So, when travelling from Balmain to Circular Quay, the passenger boarded the ferry, travelled to Circular Quay and then paid a penny to pass out of the turnstiles.

At the Circular Quay entry there was a notice-board that said:

"Notice. A fare of one penny must be paid on entering or leaving the wharf. No exception will be made to this rule, whether the passenger has travelled by the ferry or not."

In this case, Mr Robertson (a Sydney solicitor) entered the wharf at Circular Quay, paid the penny and passed through the turnstile. When he got to the wharf, the ferry had left, but instead of waiting for the next one he decided to catch another company's ferry which left from a different wharf. He tried to leave the wharf, but refused to pay the penny to get out again. He was restrained by staff, but he eventually overpowered them and got out. He sued the ferry company for wrongful imprisonment and assault.

This case was heard in the Supreme Court, then went on appeal to the High Court, and finally to the Privy Council.

The real argument became: was the notice above the entry effective to absolve the ferry company from having to carry Mr Robertson and enable it to demand payment of the second penny, for the stated purpose of leaving the wharf?

The Privy Council held that the notice did apply in that way to Mr Robertson because he was a regular user and should have been aware of the words, even though he might not have actually read them.

Mr Robertson lost the case and not only had to pay the second penny, but also 10,000 pounds in legal costs to the ferry company — a great deal of money in 1906.

Source: Cordato, A, "Australian Travel and Tourism Law"

Often, express terms are written into the contract, and implied terms are implied from the surrounding circumstances, for example, the quality of the hotel rooms if the contract is undertaken at the hotel lobby. If the lobby area is elegant and luxurious, one may assume that the rooms will be of a similar standard.

The book, Australian Travel and Tourism Law by Anthony Cordato, provides many case studies that illustrate the finer points of contract law. the Box contains a summary of one of the most famous and often-quoted cases, that of The Balmain New Ferry Co Ltd v Robertson:

This case set a precedent for a contract of carriage in ferry travel that can be used in other forms of travel today, where tokens, tickets or even vouchers are used. Any conditions that form part of the contract must be brought to the attention of the traveller before the contract becomes binding, usually before the tour has started, or arrival at a hotel, for example. However, in the case study, the contract became binding when the token was used to pass through the turnstile, not when it was bought. So, the notice on the wall was considered to provide enough information on the conditions of travel before entering the wharf through the turnstile.

It was ruled in this case that Mr Robertson would have seen the sign many times, and therefore been aware of the conditions, however this is an area that can be (and often is) contested. This case shows the importance of checking that your customers are aware of all terms and conditions related to the given contract, either by pointing out a sign or the conditions on the back of a ticket.

An area that follows closely on from contract law and consumer protection, is the tourism operation's legal liability towards the general public, or public liability.

Public Liability

A tourism operator can be held legally liable for injury to a member of the general public, and it is compulsory for all businesses to have some form of public liability insurance cover. Companies also need this cover to protect them from the costs of compensation, as without it, one large claim could easily force a company into insolvency. In some cases a company's liability can be limited, or restricted to certain situations. Some of the more common examples of are examined in this chapter.

In New Zealand, the Accident Rehabilitation and Compensation Insurance Scheme (ACC) covers visitors as well as New Zealanders for accidents. New Zealand employers and employees pay levies to support the scheme, similar to Australia's compulsory Third Party Insurance on motor vehicles, but with a far broader application. Appendix Three contains contact details for the ACC.

When is a Business Liable?

If an injury is caused by operator negligence, the operator will be considered responsible. For example, if your tourism product includes horse riding and a client falls off and breaks an arm, you may have behaved negligently if you failed to determine that the person had never ridden before, and put them on a horse that needed an experienced rider. However, if the client indicated that they were experienced and aware of the dangers of horse riding, you may not be found to be negligent, and therefore not liable.

Areas Covered by Public Liability

Public liability relates to any area that involves the general public, such as the:
- safety of buildings and their surrounds;
- safety of any activities undertaken by the public (from high risk adventure activities to putting a log on a campfire).

For example, if someone walks into your premises and trips over a piece of carpet that has lifted, you will probably be found liable under public liability. Even if the person is outside your premises when a loose brick falls off the building and injures them, you are also liable. The person does not have to be a client, just a member of the "general public".

Your Liability on Government Land

If your business operates on publicly-owned land (managed by state governments in Australia), the government requires you to sign a form releasing it from responsibility for any accidents or injuries incurred on your tour. The land management agencies also require any tourism operator who is running their business on land or premises managed by the government to hold public liability insurance.

For example, all tour operators using land managed by the Department of Natural Resources and Environment in Victoria must have at leat $5 million of public liability insurance cover before they get a permit to operate on that land. This is the case in most states.

A number of Acts relate to the area of public liability for nature-based, ecotourism and adventure tour operators. These include:

New Zealand
> Treaty of Waitangi
> Resource Management Act 1991
> Conservation Act 1987
> Forests Amendment Act 1993
> National Parks Act 1980
> Reserves Act 1977
> Marine Reserves Act 1971

Victoria
>National Parks Act 1975
>Forests Act 1958
>Land Act 1958
>Crown Land (Reserves) Act 1978

Queensland
>Nature Conservation Act 1992
>National Parks and Wildlife Act 1975

South Australia
>National Parks and Wildlife Act 1975

Liability insurance provides you with protection against the consequences of being held legally liable for loss, damage or injury to the public. So, it is important (as well as compulsory in many areas) that all tourism operators have a form of public liability insurance.

Limiting Liability (Australia)

In some cases it is possible to limit the extent of your liability by introducing exclusion clauses in brochures and contracts. An exclusion clause is a statement that says the tourism operator "will not be held responsible if .... happens". This usually relates to natural disasters, changeable weather, or any other thing that you do not have direct control over that may affect the quality of your product.

In legal terms, these clauses must be:
- clear in meaning, and
- certain in effect

Basically, this means that any exemption clause included in your brochure must be clear, and the customer is aware of it, and able to understand it. The tourism operator or agent should ensure that customers are aware of all clauses before they sign any contract/booking.

As mentioned above, many governments require tourism operators to indemnify them against legal action. They are limiting their liability by making the tourism operator responsible for what happens on the public land that they manage.

If the customer does not fully understand what they are reading, even if they sign the form it may not hold up in court. Therefore, it is extremely important to have any forms like this written in "plain English" — in a way that everyone can understand, without affecting the legal standing of the document.

Special Note: Always get legal advice if you are involved in this area in your work, and do not use these examples without such advice.

Example: Disclaimer Of Liability

1 I ("The Customer") hereby agree to provide the Tour Operator ("Tour Operator") named in this tour voucher with a complete release from any and all claims of any nature whatsoever which may but for this disclaimer of liability have as a consequence of or in any way relating to the services provided by the Tour Operator and waiver of liability to the Tour Operator listed overleaf.

2 The Customer acknowledges that participation in the activity offered by the Tour Operator is by its nature inherently dangerous, and that, except to the extent provided under any legislation, The Customer releases the Tour Operator from any and all claims, liability costs and demands and agrees not to sue the Tour Operator or its officers, employees, agents and independent contractors for any personal injury, death, property damage or other loss of any nature whatsoever sustained by The Customer as a result of the participation in and use of facilities of the Tour Operator or due to any cause whatsoever and including negligence at common law on the part of the Tour Operator, its officers, employees, agents and independent contractors, and The Customer agrees to indemnify the Tour Operator against any claims brought by The Customer or any other person on behalf of The Customer in respect of such injury, loss or damage.

3 The Customer also agrees to indemnify the Tour Operator against any claim made by any other person whomsoever against the Tour Operator in respect of any damage, loss or injury arising out of the presence of The Customer on the Tour Operator's property or use of Tour Operator's facilities by The Customer.

4 In undertaking this activity, and signing this Disclaimer of Liability The Customer is not relying on any oral, written or visual representation or statements made by the Tour Operator or its employees, servants and agents and that there has been no inducement or coercion by the Tour Operator.

Source: On-Track Tourism Consultants

European Union (EC) Directive

All segments of the tourism industry that involve organising, advising or guiding customers must adhere to various areas of the Trade Practices Act, Occupational Health and Safety Act and under Common Law, in particular the law of contract. However, moves are being made to formalise this wide range of laws and Acts into a single form of legislation specifically designed for tourism operations. The European Union Directive, known as the EC Directive, has been developed by European countries in an attempt to achieve this. The EC Directive is being considered all around the world and may be the first of many similar types of legislation.

It is important to understand the Directive as it can affect tourism operations in Australia and New Zealand. It relates to package travel arranged in European Union countries, and holds the European agent liable for any contraventions of the Directive by the tour provider.

The aims of the Directive are to:
- Provide a minimum uniform standard for package travel;
- Protect consumers and compensate them if their plans are interrupted, or if the operator is insolvent.

What this means is that any tour operator, accommodation provider or wholesaler who promotes their product in Europe must follow certain requirements — responsibility rests solely with the organiser and/or retailer. The term "package" is defined here as being a combination of any two or more of: transport, accommodation and other tour services, involving a period of 24 hours or more.

The major area of interest here is the requirements for brochures, which must include the following information:
- price
- destination
- means of transport
- type and location of accommodation
- meal plan
- itinerary
- passport and visa requirement
- payment details
- minimum number for tour

The organiser must also provide the customer with all transport details and a local representative in the countries visited.

The EC Directive imposes a strict responsibility, or "no-fault liability" upon the organiser and/or retailer of package travel. The advantage to the consumer is that they do not have to cope with a foreign legal system — they can lodge a claim directly against the organiser and/or retailer.

If European tourists are part of your market (and they are a big nature-based tourism sector), it is important that you understand the EC Directive. If in doubt, seek legal advice.

Conclusion

Understanding the tourism industry's distribution system will enable operators to plan and utilise it to their best advantage. Using the services of intermediaries is essential in developing your product, and even if you believe that you will take all reservations direct from the general public, it is important to be aware of, and to take into acount, relevant commission rates when deciding on your initial costing. An extremely cost-effective method of marketing and utilising the distribution system is to package your product with other related goods and services.

Ecotourism

There are a range of legal considerations that relate to tourism operations, from the Trade Practices Act to the EC Directive. An awareness and basic understanding of such considerations is crucial to any business, particularly areas of liability and legal responsibility.

References and Further Reading

Australian Conservation Foundation, Australian Council of Trade Unions and Commonwealth Department of Employment, Education and Training (1994), **Green Jobs in Industry, Research Report**, Melbourne, Australia

This report has a significant chapter on ecotourism, covering ecotourism from a conservation viewpoint, focussing on the employment benefits of ecotourism.

Australian Institute of Travel and Tourism and New Zealand Institute of Travel and Tourism (1996), **Australian and New Zealand Tourism Professional**, National Publishing Group, New South Wales, Australia

The official journal of AITT and NZITT provides articles and information on tourism in both Australia and New Zealand. Ecotourism and nature based tourism features in many articles. It was used for background information and to identify case studies.

Australian Tourism Industry Association (1990), **Environmental Guidelines for Tourist Developments**, Canberra, Australia

Although this booklet is a few years old, it is a good introduction to environmental aspects of development and has a range of valuable checklists and guidelines. The author, the Australian Tourism Industry Association is now known as the Tourism Council Australia (TCA).

Back, Chris (1995), *Rottnest Island*, in **Sustainable Tourism, An Australian Perspective**, editors Rob Harris and Neil Leiper, Butterworth Heinemann, Australia, pp 27-33

This case study has been referred to in the book.

Bates, John (1991), **Planning for Tourism and Major Developments: Issues Affecting Local Government, Tourism Information Paper No. 1**, Second Edition, New South Wales Tourism Commission

A short report which focuses mainly on local government's role in the tourism development process. It could be an interesting background document for anyone submitting a proposal to local government, particularly in New South Wales. Its scope, however, is very general and introductory.

Blamey, R.K. (1995), **The Nature of Ecotourism**, Occasional Paper No. 21, Bureau of Tourism Research, Canberra Australia

A research publication which helps to define ecotourism and profile the ecotourist as well as discussing the significance of ecotourism. It promises a great deal, and presents a good array of research data, but does not analyse it fully, leaving that to the reader. It illustrates that much more long-term research is needed, and spends many pages discussing a definition in relation to market research. Great for students and consultants, but may be a bit heavy-going for operators.

Much of the relevant data has been used in the background of the book, and tables used as quoted.

Boele, Nicolette (1996), **Tourism Switched On, Sustainable Energy Technologies of the Australian Tourism Industry**, presented by Tourism Council Australia, World Travel and Tourism Environment Research Centre, Office of National Tourism, Australia.

A comprehensive guide to energy technologies which provides strong tourism case studies on most technologies. Available from the Office of National Tourism in Canberra free of charge, it is a good starting point when looking at sustainable energy.

Used as a background reference in the book and to clarify a few points in a less technical manner.

Charters, Tony (1995), *Kingfisher Bay Resort and Village*, in **Sustainable Tourism, An Australian Perspective**, editors Rob Harris and Neil Leiper, Butterworth Heinemann, Australia, pp 117-124

This case study has been referred to in the book.

Centre for Coastal Management (1996), **Environmental Guidelines for Tourism Planning and Management in the Coastal Zone of Australia**, Centre for Tourism, Southern Cross University, Lismore, NSW, Australia

This is a background paper to the "Coastal Tourism: Guiding Principles for Sustainable Development" draft paper produced by Prosser et al. It provides a number of case studies and basic environmental information.

Used as a background resource and to identify additional case studies.

Commonwealth Department of Tourism (1994a), **National Ecotourism Strategy**, Australia

With the change of government in Australia in 1996, this publication is no longer the "official" government strategy. However, it provides a thorough introduction to the concept of ecotourism and is often referred to.

Commonwealth Department of Tourism (1994b), **A Guide to Innovative Technology for Sustainable Tourism**, Australia

Produced for the Sustainable Design and Ecotourism Seminar held in Tasmania in 1994, this introductory booklet looks at water and energy conservation, waste minimisation and appropriate building materials.

Commonwealth Department of Tourism (1995), **Best Practice Ecotourism, A guide to energy waste and waste minimisation**, Australia

>An excellent publication that provides plenty of case studies as working examples of energy and waste minimisation in the areas of transport, energy supply and efficiency, heating and cooling; lighting, solid materials, building materials, toilets, cooking, cleaning, washing, newspaper, cardboard, glass and plastics, office equipment and paper.

>This publication has been referred to extensively in the book.

Commonwealth Department of Tourism (1996), **Directory of Ecotourism Education**, Australia

>A comprehensive listing of courses, seminars and other ecotourism educational programs being run in Australia. Some of the programs no longer operate and others have a very limited ecotourism content, but it is a good resource and indicates the range of interest in this field.

>The directory was used as a background resource.

Cordato, A.J. (1993), **Australian Travel and Tourism Law**, Second Edition, Butterworths, Australia

>The main legal text used in most tourism training programs. It covers all areas relating to legal aspects of tourism in a relatively readable form, with many of the case studies that set the legal precedents we now operate under. A good reference, and has been used in the legal sections of this book.

Country Victoria Tourism Council (1995), **Why Should Local Governments Invest in Tourism?**, CVTC Inc., Melbourne

>Designed for local governments, this publication covers all aspects of the industry in a very broad sense as well as outlining local government's role. It should be mandatory reading for all local government management and staff. It is an excellent introductory publication, and as such has been used for background information.

Cox Inall Communications Pty Ltd (1996), **Cultivating Rural Tourism**, Australia

>An initiative funded by the Federal Government under the Rural Tourism Program, this exellent publication includes a video, booklet and a range of fact sheets. It includes numerous case studies and examples which could be incorporated into a combined ecotourism/rural tourism product.

>This publication has been referred to extensively in the book, particularly when looking at extending ecotourism into other rural concerns.

Crabtree, Alice (1995), *Quicksilver Connections*, in **Sustainable Tourism, An Australian Perspective**, editors Rob Harris and Neil Leiper, Butterworth Heinemann, Australia pp 145-154

>This case study has been referred to in the book.

Craik, J (1991), **Resorting to Tourism - Cultural policies for tourist development in Australia**, Allen and Unwin Pty Ltd, Australia

>Concentrating mainly on the academic issues of tourism development, this book has an interesting section on environmental management that has been used as background information.

Department of Conservation (1996), **Visitor Strategy**, Wellington, New Zealand
> An overview of conservation and tourism on New Zealand public land managed by the Department of Conservation. A section on managing tourism concessions relates directly to any tourism business that operates on or near protected lands.

Department of Industry, Science and Tourism (1996), **Projecting Success, Visitor Management Projects for Sustainable Tourism Growth**, Canberra, Australia
> A profile of 21 projects undertaken by various land management agencies throughout Australia. While it relates mainly to larger-scale public land management, many of the issues and solutions can be converted to a smaller, private scale. An easy-to-read publication which provides interesting anecdotes of other areas, their problems and solutions that may be used in a guided tour.
>
> The outcomes of some of these projects have been referred to in the book, and some of the case studies used as examples of site management.

Dickman, S (1995), **Marketing Your Tourism Business**, Tourism Training Victoria, Australia
> A kit incorporating a manual and two videos ("Marketing your tourism business", and "Understanding the inbound market") with many case studies and practical information. It relates to a general tourism business, but the theory is the same for ecotourism businesses, and has been used as a general information source.

Economic Research Services (1992), **Report on the Economic Contribution of Tourism to the Daintree/Cape Tribulation Area**, Cairns, Australia
> This report gives some indication of the range of economic benefits that tourism based on the attractions of a natural area can bring to the local community and region.
>
> It has been used in the book to provide some of the facts in relation to the economic benefits of nature-based tourism.

Ecotourism Association of Australia (1995-7), **Newsletters**, Australia
> The EAA's newsletters provide a range of excellent information on current issues and trends in ecotourism as well as highlighting some case studies in each edition. The newsletters are available to members of the association and are a great source of information.
>
> Used as a general resource and for case studies in the book.

Ecotourism Association of Australia (1996), **Australian Ecotourism Guide, 1996**, Australia
> Another publication available to members and others (for a fee), it provides a listing of all EAA members with descriptions of many of their operations, relevant information and case studies. A great resource for anyone wishing to find out what the state of ecotourism is in Australia.
>
> Used as a general resource, a contact point and for case studies in the book.

Ecotourism Association of Australia (1996), **Strategic Alliances: Ecotourism Partnerships in Practice**, Conference Papers form the EAA National Conference, 14-17 November 1996, Kangaroo Island, South Australia.

A number of the papers have been used as case studies and in reference to working with communities and the government in various partnerships. Specific papers have been listed separately in the References.

Ecotourism Association of Australia and Australian Tourism Operators Association (1996), **National Ecotourism Accreditation Program**, Australia

Provides accreditation standards for ecotourism operators, accommodation and attractions, looking at interpretation, sustainability, local community involvement, satisfaction and marketing.

These standards have been referred to extensively in the book, with all aspects relating to ecotourism accreditation covered.

Harris, R and Leiper, N (eds) (1995), **Sustainable Tourism, an Australian Perspective**, Butterworth-Heinemann, Australia

A good overview of sustainable tourism, incorporating ecotourism, with case studies written by tour operators, government departments and management authorities. It is easy to follow and will be of interest to those wanting further case studies and general information.

This reference has been used for some of the case studies presented in the book — individual references written by people other than the editors are listed in this section under the author's names.

Harris, R and Varga, D (1995), *Jemby-Rinjah Lodge*, in **Sustainable Tourism, An Australian Perspective**, editors Rob Harris and Neil Leiper, Butterworth Heinemann, Australia, pp 109-116

This case study has been referred to in the book.

La Planche, S (1995), **Stepping Lightly on Australia**, Angus and Robertson, Australia

A guide primarily for independent travellers, with details on activities and natural areas in Australia and relevant ecotourism operators. It could be of some use in identifying what tourists (or Ms. La Planche) consider to be of interest from an environmental point of view, and how this may compare with your own region.

Lee, Tony (1995), *Australis: Soft adventure natural history tours*, in **Sustainable Tourism, An Australian Perspective**, editors Rob Harris and Neil Leiper, Butterworth Heinemann, Australia, pp 135-139

This case study has been referred to in the book.

Manidis Roberts Consultants (1996), **Developing a Tourism Optimisation Management Model (TOMM), A model to monitor and manage tourism on Kangaroo Island**, Consultation Draft Report, Australia

A draft report looking at establishing standards (benchmarks) to measure all aspects of tourism in a nature-based environment. Good overview of the areas that affect ecotourism design, development and implementation.

McKercher, Bob (1998), **The Business of Nature-Based Tourism**, Hospitality Press, Melbourne

A recent publication that covers the business planning aspects of starting and operating a tourism business, with emphasis on ecotourism and nature-based tourism. It goes into a little more detail in relation to the business aspects, such as developing a business plan, budgets and cash flows. A good companion to this book.

Moscardo, G., Morrison, A.M., Pearce, P.L., (1996), *Specialist Accommodation and Ecologically-Sustainable Tourism*, in **Journal of Sustainable Tourism**, Vol.4, No. 3, 1996

Written by an American and two Australian academics (Moscardo and Pearce), this article it has a strong Australian focus and has been used when looking at existing accommodation. Used mainly as a background resource paper.

New Zealand Tourism Board (1998), **Strategic Plan**, New Zealand

The NZTB has produced a glossy brochure outlining its strategic plan to develop New Zealand as "The Best Holiday Left on Earth". This is a concise summary of the Board's goals and should be read and re-read by any person involved in tourism in New Zealand.

New Zealand Tourism Board (1998), **Southern Lakes Tourism Strategy**, New Zealand

A good strategy that provides infrastructure, land use and marketing strategies for the region that can, in many cases, be modified to individual operators as well as providing a big picture view. Used as a background resource and to provide overall New Zealand tourism information.

New Zealand Tourism Board (1997), **Stewart Island Tourism Strategy**, New Zealand

Some good information on handling tourism in an enclosed, island environment, it outlines the problems, issues and recommends strategies to handle them. While this is an overall strategy, it contains numerous points that are also relevant to individual operators. It is also a good community-based tourism document.

New Zealand Tourist Board & New Zealand Tourism Industry Association (1996), **Tourism's Guide to the Resource Management Act**, NZTB, New Zealand

An excellent publication that is easy to read and extremely informative. Information is provided on the Resource Management Act and the various processes required to obtain resource consents as required by the Act. However, it goes beyond merely outlining these procedures, providing constructive suggestions on handling environmental issues and the public consultation process. Some of the case studies in the publication have been used as examples of New Zealand operations, particularly in Chapters 3 and 5.

O'Reilly, Bernard (undated, circa 1940), **Green Mountains and Cullenbong**, Kemp Place Investments, Brisbane, Australia

Heritage information for the case studies on O'Reilly's Guest House, this is a great book to read for enjoyment as well as its place in our heritage.

O'Reilly, Peter S. (1996), *Sex, Love and Strategic Alliances*, in **Strategic Alliances: Ecotourism Partnerships in Practice**, Conference Papers from the EAA National Conference, 14-17 November 1996, Kangaroo Island, South Australia, pp.35-39

Case studies on incorporating non-indigenous heritage and the environment as well as simple marketing and guiding techniques.

Plumridge, T., James, R., Whitelaw, P., Curlewis, A., Cock P., Pfueller, S. (1996), *Ecotourist Profiles at Halls Gap*, in **Strategic Alliances: Ecotourism Partnerships in Practice**, Conference Papers form the EAA National Conference, 14-17 November 1996, Kangaroo Island, South Australia, pp.55-60

Presented at the EAA conference, this paper is among the few attempts to profile the ecotourism market in an Australian context. The research project was supported by a grant from the Federal Government through the National Ecotourism Strategy. It has been used as a case study in Chapter 2.

Preece, Noel (1995), *Discovery Ecotours: Sustainable Tourism in Outback Australia*, in **Sustainable Tourism, An Australian Perspective**, editors Rob Harris and Neil Leiper, Butterworth Heinemann, Australia, pp 140-144

This case study has been referred to in the book.

Prosser, G., Davis, D., Knox S., Luckie K (1996), **Coastal Tourism: Guiding Principles for Sustainable Development, Draft**, Southern Cross University, NSW

A draft paper that has been useful in identifying some of the issues particular to coastal environments and ecotourism as well as recommending further publications for more detail.

Generally used as a background document, and referring to a few points regarding coastal and marine development.

Richardson, Janet (1993), **Ecotourism and Nature-based Holidays**, Choice Books, Marrickville, Australia

This was one of the first publications that attempted to define and identify ecotourism products in Australia. Due to data being obtained from a self-completion questionnaire with some very broad categories and leading questions, some of the products do not truly come under an "eco" category, however it provides an interesting inventory and introduction to ecotourism in Australia. It is geared more towards the consumer than the provider, and as such provides some insights into what the tourist may be looking for in an ecotourism experience. Used as a background resource.

Richins, Harold (1995), *Decision Making and Community Commitment in a Coastal Tourism Region*, in **Proceedings of the National Tourism and Hospitality Conference, 1995**, Melbourne, pp.177-193

This paper looks at a coastal community (Port Stephens) and its tourism decision-making process. It has been used as background information, and as a case study, and provides some insight into this complex area.

Richins, Harold (1996), *Tourism Decision Making in Local Communities: Constraints and Impacts*, in **Tourism and Hospitality Research - Australian and International Perspectives**, Proceedings from the Australian Tourism and Hospitality Research Conference, Coffs Harbour 1996 pp.71-81

A research paper that looks at the decision-making process of local councils, in an attempt to understand issues surrounding councillors' decisions to help future tourism operators in gaining council approval for their projects. This is an extremely complex area, and the paper provides some valuable insights that have been incorporated into the book, however the research being undertaken is in its early stages, and further results will provide more information.

Roberts, Brian (1992), **Land Care Manual**, University of New South Wales Press, Sydney, Australia

> An overview of Land Care and the issues involved, which although it is a few years old offers much practical information and advice on dealing with land degradation and the aims of Land Care. The book is an easy-to-read introduction to Land Care as well as a resource for experienced "carers" to refer to.
>
> Used to provide a link between Land Care and ecotourism.

Sutton, Mark and Bates, Badger (1996), *Mootwingee National Park - Western NSW: A History of Cooperative Tourism Management*, in **Strategic Alliances: Ecotourism Partnerships in Practice**, Conference Papers from the EAA National Conference, 14-17 November 1996, Kangaroo Island, South Australia, pp. attachments

> Used as one of the case studies on indigenous communities, this paper shows the progression from land claim through to independent management.

Tasmania Department of Tourism, Sport and Recreation (1994), **Ecotourism, Adding Value to Tourism in Natural Areas**, Tasmania

Tasmania Department of Tourism, Sport and Recreation (1994), **Nature-based Tourism in Tasmania - A Profile of Visitors**, Occasional Paper 5/94, Tasmania

Tasmania Department of Tourism, Sport and Recreation (1994), **Contribution of Tourism to the Tasmanian Economy**, Occasional Paper 6/94, Tasmania

> As Tasmania relies heavily on its natural environment for most tourism activities, all the Tasmanian publications provided valuable background information, but some information is a bit dated.

Tourism New South Wales (1995), **Farm Tourism - What Should I Know?**, Sydney, Australia

> An introductory information guide on Farm Tourism, used to integrate farm and ecotourism, mainly as a background document.

Tourism Training Australia (1996), **Tour Guiding Competency Standards - Draft**, Sydney Australia, unpublished

> Provides competency standards for general and specialist ecotourism guides that can be used in training and developing ecotourism products and staff. Used as a background document as it is still in draft format. The final competencies will be available in late 1998/9.

Tourism Victoria (undated, circa 1994/5), **Building Tourism - Guidelines for Tourism Development in Victoria**, Australia

> An easy-to-follow step by step program for developments in the state, from the concept through to planning and development approval and implementation. It is not only environmentally based, and provides information on feasibility assessment, business planning and obtaining finance. Although it does relate specifically to Victoria, it has a great deal of general information that would be of benefit to all. Overall, an excellent publication on tourism development, both large and small scale.

Tourism Victoria (1996), **International Markets Update, 28 November 1996**, Tourism Victoria, Melbourne, Australia

> A copy of papers presented at a seminar of the same name held each year by Tourism Victoria and the Victorian Tourism Operators Association. The seminar and notes are an excellent source for any Victorian tourism operator who is involved (or thinking of become involved) in international tourism markets. It has been used in the book in a general way when looking at international marketing.

United States Department of the Interior (1993), **Guiding Principles of Sustainable Design**, USA

> Discusses means for achieving sustainability in parks and conservation areas in relation to ecotourism. Many of the principles can be applied to private enterprise.

Walmsley, John (1996), *Conservation and Tourism - Achieving Million Dollar Partnerships*, in **Strategic Alliances: Ecotourism Partnerships in Practice**, Conference Papers form the EAA National Conference, 14-17 November 1996, Kangaroo Island, South Australia, pp.19-24

> An interesting and controversial paper presented at the EAA conference. Dr. Walmsley's successes indicate the potential of ecotourism and conservation. Provides some interesting case study information that has been referred to in the book.

Weaver, D., Glenn, C., Rounds, R. (1996), *Private Ecotourism Operations in Manitoba, Canada*, in **Journal of Sustainable Tourism**, Vol.4, No. 3, 1996

> One of very few references to look at private sector site providers of ecotourism, but it is only a general reference in researching the potential of private sites. Many of the problems identified by operators in Manitoba have already been addressed in Australia, such as forming networks and associations to deal with government issues, education and marketing.

Wight, Pamela W., (1996a), *North American Ecotourists: Market Profile and Trip Characteristics,* in **Journal of Travel Research**, Vol. 34, No. 4, Spring 1996, Colorado

Wight, Pamela W., (1996b), *North American Ecotourism Markets: Motivations, Preferences and Destinations,* in **Journal of Travel Research**, Vol. 35, No. 1, Summer 1996, Colorado

> These two articles look at the North American ecotourism market, and were useful when considering what makes up the "ecotourist" profile. As ecotourists from North America travel to Australia, this profile is of interest to us. The research conducted looked at markets, trip characteristics, motivation, preferences and demand. Relevant details have been incorporated into the book.

Appendix 1

Codes of Practice and Tips for Operators

The PATA Code for Environmentally Responsible Tourism

The PATA (Pacific Asia Tourism Association) Code urges Association and Chapter members and their industry partners to:

- Adopt the necessary practices to conserve the environment, including the use of renewable resources in a sustainable manner and the conservation of non-renewable resources.

- Contribute to the conservation of any habitat of flora and fauna, and of any site whether natural or cultural, which may be affected by tourism.

- Encourage relevant authorities to identify areas worthy of conservation and to determine the level of development, if any, which would ensure those areas are conserved.

- Ensure that assessment procedures recognise the cumulative, as well as the individual, effects of all developments on the environment.

- Comply with all international conventions in relation to the environment.

- Comply with all national. state and local laws concerning the environment.

- Encourage those involved in tourism to comply with local, regional, and national planning policies and to participate in the planning process.

- Provide the opportunity for the wider community to take part in discussions and consultations on tourism planning issues insofar as they affect the tourism industry and the community.

- Acknowledge responsibility for the environmental impacts of all tourism-related projects and activities and undertake all necessary changes to those practices.

- Foster environmentally responsible practices including waste management, recycling and energy use.

- Foster in both management and staff, of all tourism-related projects and activities, an awareness of environmental and conservation principles.

Support the inclusion of professional conservation principles in tourism education, training and planning.

Encourage an understanding by all those involved in tourism of each community's customs, cultural values, beliefs and traditions, and how they relate to the environment.

Enhance the appreciation and understanding by tourists of the environment through the provision of accurate information and appropriate interpretation.

Establish detailed environmental policies and/or guidelines for the various sectors of the tourism industry.

The Ecotourism Association of Australia Code of Practice

- Strengthen the conservation effort for, and enhance the natural integrity of, the places visited
- Respect the sensitivities of other cultures
- Be efficient in the use of natural resources eg. water, energy
- Ensure waste disposal has minimal environmental and aesthetic impacts
- Develop a recycling program
- Support principals (i.e. hotels, carriers etc) who have a conservation ethic
- Keep abreast of current political and environmental issues, particularly of the local area
- Network with other stakeholders (particularly those in the local area) to keep each other informed of developments and to encourage the use of this Code of Practice
- Endeavour to use distribution networks (eg. catalogues) and retail outlets to raise environmental awareness by distributing guidelines to consumers
- Support ecotourism education /training for guides and managers
- Employ tour guides well versed and respectful of local cultures and environments
- Give clients appropriate verbal and written educational material (interpretation) and guidance with respect to the natural and cultural history of the areas visited
- Use locally produced goods that benefit the local community, but do not buy goods made from threatened or endangered species
- Never intentionally disturb or encourage the disturbance of wildlife or wildlife habitats
- Keep vehicles to designated roads and trails
- Abide by the rules and regulations applying in natural areas
- Commit to the principle of best practice
- Comply with Australian safety standards
- Ensure truth in advertising, and
- Maximise the quality of experience for hosts and guests.

Environmental Tourism Tips from PATA Green Leaf Members of the Month

(Reproduced from PATA Internet site with permission)

Each issue of the PATA "UpDate" newsletter features a PATA Green Leaf Member of the Month — a PATA Green Leaf participant who demonstrates outstanding commitment to the PATA Code for Environmentally Responsible Tourism. Following are environmental tips from previous PATA Green Leaf Members of the Month. These suggestions can be adopted by all travel and tourism industry members to help protect cultural and natural resources.

Ideas from Environmental Hotels of Auckland
New Zealand Tourism Board
Green Leaf Member of the Month: June 1997

1　Plant native species — they have good all-year colour and consume less water (reduces pesticide use also).

2　Encourage your suppliers to pack goods in returnable, reusable plastic crates.

3　Buy recycled — close the recycling loop.

4　Reduce water temperatures in laundry to 60 degrees C. Set water heaters at a standard temperature degrees C.

5　Incorporate an environmental section within your induction training program.

Green Operational Tips From Maupintour
Maupintour, Lawrence, Kansas, USA
Green Leaf Member of the Month: March 1997

1　Maupintour's clientele are educated and aware of the importance of protecting the environment. They are involved and influential in their communities and speak out on behalf of conservation.

2　Group size is small in sensitive areas, usually around 20 to 25.

3　Groups are always escorted by knowledgeable local guides and are managed by professional tour managers.

4　Maupintour uses hundreds of hotels and ground operators throughout the world, most of whom are keenly interested in protecting their own "turf" because it directly impacts their livelihood.

5　Excursions into sensitive areas are always day trips. Meals and accommodation are outside of the protected habitats, consequently no destruction or waste is left behind.

6　The cruise lines Maupintour works with, such as Holland America Line, are very aware of proper treatment of the environment and enforce strict adherence to their code of "leaving nothing behind except a wake."

A Few Green Tips from Brian Boru
Brian Boru Hotel, Thames, New Zealand
Green Leaf Member of the Month: January 1997

1 Use environmentally sound cleaning agents in refillable containers.
2 Use organic pesticides only.
3 Washing machines with high-speed spin will ensure a maximum reduction in water.
4 Recycle office equipment such as toner, disks and paper.
5 Use water-saving sterilisers for dishes and glasses; use dishwasher only when full.
6 Avoid wrapping foods in plastic film and don't use Styrofoam.
7 Eliminate all single-serve packaging.
8 Use fabric napkins.

Miraval's Suggestions for Guests
Miraval, Life in Balance, Catalina, Arizona, USA
Green Leaf Member of the Month: July 1996

1 Take a five-minute shower instead of a bath. This saves close to 13 gallons of water per shower.
2 Fill sink basin with water when shaving instead of letting water run continuously. You will save about three gallons of water with every shave.
3 Use hair dryers on "low heat" setting; it saves energy and is better for your hair.
4 Phone-in room service orders instead of writing them on an order card.
5 Close curtains when leaving room to alleviate energy use needed to keep room cool.
6 When hiking, stay on marked trails.
7 Use refillable water bottles.

Inter-Continental Hotels' Tips for a Greener Hotel
Inter-Continental Hotel Group, Asia-Pacific, Sydney, Australia
Green Leaf Member of the Month: May 1996

1 Waste Management: Recycle bottle corks to make cricket balls, floor tiles, etc. From recycling proceeds, the Inter-Continental Hotel Sydney has contributed A$18,000 to a war veterans retirement village for the purchase of wheelchairs.
2 Energy: Install sub-metering for electricity, gas and water, then make each department accountable for its consumption.
3 Product Purchase: Use a supplier questionnaire to ensure that the items purchased are environmentally friendly.
4 Indoor Air Quality: Follow a preventive maintenance programme for all air handling units, including filters and heating and cooling coils.
5 Air Emissions: Institute a refrigerant management plan including reclaiming and recycling of gases and leak detection.
6 Noise: Install proper door seals and double glaze windows of guest and function rooms.

7 Storage Tanks: Inspect fuel and gas tanks regularly for leaks; shutoff valves must be working properly.

8 Asbestos: Carry out an asbestos check and plan for correct removal of any asbestos.

9 PCBs: Check transformers and fluorescent fittings for PCBs, which become toxic in the case of a fire.

10 Pesticides/Herbicides: Ensure that all chemicals are environmentally friendly, properly stored and labelled.

11 Hazardous Materials: Identify all hazardous materials; establish correct storage and handling procedures.

12 Water: Use all cold water storage tanks continuously wherever possible to avoid stagnant water problems and minimise chemical water treatment.

13 Community Action/Innovation: Encourage staff to contribute suggestions; some hotels have initiated a staff-driven environmental awards program.

14. Laundry/Dry Cleaning: Install automatic dosing systems to control chemicals and washing temperatures.

Canadian Pacific Hotels & Resorts' 16-Point Action Plan
Canadian Pacific Hotels & Resorts, Toronto, Canada
Green Leaf Member of the Month, Americas Division: September 1995

1 Set target for a 50 per cent reduction in landfill waste and a 20 per cent reduction in paper use.

2 Re-distribute and/or recycle all used soap and amenities.

3 Establish programs at all properties to recycle the following: paper, newspaper, cans, organic waste, motor oils, cardboard, plastics, bottles, coat hangers and printer cartridges.

4 Establish a policy and procedure for the identification and disposal of hazardous waste.

5 Initiate a "phase out" program to reduce or eliminate the use of the following items in CPH&R restaurants and cafeterias: individual packages of sugar, creamer and condiments and disposable cups.

6 Introduce "blue boxes" for collection of recyclable materials in guest rooms.

7 Initiate a retrofit of all appropriate lighting from incandescent to compact fluorescent bulbs at all properties.

8 Replace all shower heads and taps with low-flow alternatives.

9 Establish a standard temperature for the setting of all hot water tanks.

10 Establish a corporate purchasing policy that imposes, where appropriate, Environmental Choice standards as the minimum standard for purchase of and/or conversion to "environmentally friendly" products.

11 Convert all necessary paper products to unbleached kraft or recycled materials.

12 Streamline use of cleaning agents and, where available, replace with non-aerosol products; eliminate hazardous chemicals and synthetic perfumes.

13 Purchase only re-refined motor oil and re-inked printer ribbons for use at CPH&R.

14 Initiate negotiations with suppliers to eliminate and reduce packaging.

15 Initiate strategic alliance with Canadian Organic Growers to purchase organically grown foodstuffs.

16 Establish corporate policy to make toilet dams mandatory in all CPH&R toilet tanks that flush more than two gallons per flush.

Mountain Travel-Sobek's "Hard-Core Trek" Guidelines
Mountain Travel-Sobek, El Cerrito, California, USA
Green Leaf Member of the Month: July 1995

1 Use kerosene or propane stoves instead of lighting campfires.

2 Use only biodegradable soap and toiletries; showers are not encouraged on treks, as heating water requires wood-burning.

3 Bring a trowel to dig toilets and carry matches to burn used toilet paper.

4 Clients are encouraged to pick up trash along trails, and garbage is burned, not left behind.

5 In culturally sensitive areas, clients are not allowed to wear skin tight clothing or short shorts.

6 Clients are asked not to give trinkets to local communities, as this encourages begging.

7 Local staff are trained to be environmentally and culturally sensitive.

Appendix 2

SAMPLE BUSINESS PLAN FOR "ECOTOURS PTY LTD"

1.0 The Business

1.1 Core Business
"ECOTOURS" is based in Mytown, offering specialist ecotourism tour guides.

1.2 Mission Statement
ECOTOURS is committed to the professional development of ecotourism through providing quality tour guiding services to ecotourism operators, resulting in the growth, profitability and professional standing of the tourism industry.

1.3 Vision
To be regarded as a responsible, relevant and effective member of the Australian tourism industry.

1.4 Key Success Factors
Factors that are essential to the success of the business include:
- The ability to demonstrate knowledge of the requirements of the ecotourism industry and provide appropriately qualified guides;
- The ability to demonstrate knowledge of the ecotourism industry through direct involvement;
- The ability to communicate with all levels of the industry;
- The ability to operate outside standard business hours;
- The ability to provide experienced personnel at short notice.

1.5 Business Objectives

You should have at least three business objectives - this is just an example

Objective 1

To develop an excellent reputation and name in the ecotourism industry as a realistic and effective provider of guides.

Key Performance Indicators

- Increase in business from ecotourism operators
- Increase in direct contact from other tourism operators
- Increase in requests for industry advice from other sectors

Strategies

- Maintain a high industry profile through selective industry committee work
- Maintain active participation in local conservation groups and chambers of commerce
- Attend as many relevant industry functions, conferences and seminars as possible

Contingency Plans

- Develop expertise in other tourism areas such as accommodation and attractions.

1.6 Timelines to Achieve Objectives

This can be drawn up as a calendar, marking off the blocks of time you will be undertaking certain activities. Include monthly tourism association (or other groups) meetings as well as the longer-term activities.

1.7 SWOT Analysis

Strengths

Physical

- Access to sufficient funds to operate business
- Own/lease all equipment required — computer, printers, phones, answering machine, fax, desk, storage, car
- Utilising a home office — premises fully owned

Ecotourism

Human
Personal
- Industry knowledge
- Communication (written and verbal) skills
- Marketing/promotional ability
- Industry qualifications

Other
- Access to small business operators for advice
- Membership of Associations — Ecotourism Association of Australia, ITOA

Weaknesses	Strategies
• Industry reputation and profile not as prominent as desired	Take advantage of all chances to get name recognised (eg. industry newsletter and trade contributions, voluntary work)
• Undercapitalised	Obtain professional advice Limit capital needs Develop immediate cashflow
• Limited personnel resource	If unable to complete work, subcontract where possible

Opportunities
- Australians are holidaying closer to home
- Australians are also taking shorter holidays (2–7 day trips), which suits the ecotourism industry
- Ecotourism, both domestic and inbound, is a growth industry
- Governments are committing significant funds to tourism, particularly ecotourism
- The A$ exchange rate is attractive to the inbound tourist, assisting in industry growth

Threats	Strategies
• Increased competition from other providers entering the niche as they recognise the opportunities	Keep in touch with industry trends through development of rapport with clients
• Increased competition from tourism graduates	Networking in the industry

2.0 The Industry

ECOTOURS is a part of the Australian tourism industry, providing guiding services to the niche market of ecotourism.

2.1 Sources of Information

There are many sources of information in the tourism industry, the major ones being:

Industry Associations

Bureau of Tourism Research

Australian Bureau of Statistics

State/Territory Tourism Associations

Department of Conservation and
    Natural Resources

State Parliamentary Tourism Committees

Commonwealth Department of Tourism

Yellow Pages

Business Directories

Local Councils

Libraries

Regional Tourism Associations

Australian Tourist Commission

General Media and Trade Press

2.2 Industry Associations

The most relevant, active and important associations for this business are:

ATIA   Australian Tourism Industry Association

ITOA   Inbound Tourism Organisations of Australia

EAA   Ecotourism Association of Australia

ACF   Australian Conservation Foundation

ATOA   Australia Tourism Operators Association

TTA   Tourism Training Australia

PATA   Pacific Asia Tourist Association

AITT   Australian Institute of Travel and Tourism

3.0 Service and Operations Plan

3.1 Primary Service

ECOTOURS is a part of the Australian tourism industry, providing environmental guides to the niche market of ecotourism.

3.2 Secondary Services

A number of secondary services have been identified:

- Environmental and tourism research in the field by guides
- Travel writing

4.0 Marketing Plan

4.1 Market

4.1.1 Client Profile

4.2 Competitors

4.3 Marketing Strategy

5.0 Financial Information

5.1 Balance Sheets for Previous Year

5.2 Projected Cash Flow for 1997-8

5.3 Projected Balance Sheets and Break-Even Analysis 1997-8

6.0 Management

Sole Proprietor

6.1 Personal Details

Appendix 3

CONTACTS

General Tourism

New Zealand

New Zealand Tourism Board
PO Box 95
Wellington
New Zealand
    Telephone: (04) 472 8860
    Facsimile: (04) 478 1736

Tourism Policy Group
Ministry of Commerce
PO Box 1473
Wellington
New Zealand
    Telephone: (04) 472 0030

Statistics New Zealand
Auckland Office
70 Symonds Street
Private Bag 92003
    Telephone: (09) 357 2100
    Facsimile: (09) 379 0859

Wellington Office
Aorangi House
85 Molesworth Street
PO Box 2922
    Telephone: (04) 495 4600
    Facsimile: (04) 495 4610

Christchurch Office
Winchester House
64 Kilmore Street
Private Bag 4741
    Telephone: (03) 374 8700
    Facsimile: (03) 374 8864

Centre for Research Evaluation and
Social Assessment (CRESA)
PO Box 3538
Wellington
New Zealand

Accident Rehabilitation and
Compensation Insurance Scheme
(ACC)
PO Box 242
Wellington
New Zealand
    Facsimile: (04) 460 7701

Australia

Office of National Tourism
Department of Industry, Science and Tourism
GPO Box 1545
Canberra ACT 2601
 Telephone: (02) 6213 7014

Australian Tourist Commission
GPO Box 2721
Sydney NSW 2001
 Telephone: (02) 9360 1111
 Facsimile: (02) 9331 3469

Australian Bureau of Statistics
 Telephone: (02) 6252 7922
 Toll Free: 008 020 608

Bureau of Tourism Research
GPO Box 1545
Canberra ACT 2601
 Telephone: (02) 6213 7124
 Facsimile: (02) 6213 6983

Tourism Forecasting Council (TFC)
The Director
Investment and Business Development
Office of National Tourism
Department of Industry, Science and Tourism
GPO Box 1545
CANBERRA ACT 2601
 Telephone: (02) 6279 7115
 Facsimile: (02) 6279 7273:

Tourism Training Australia (TTA)
PO Box Q309
QVB PO
Sydney NSW 2000
 Telephone: (02) 9290 1055
 Facsimile: (02) 9290 1001

Sydney Organising Committee for the Olympic Games (SOCOG)
PO Box 2000
Sydney NSW 2001
 Telephone: (02) 9931 2000
 Facsimile: (02) 9931 1490

Tourism Industry Bodies

Pacific Asia Travel Association (PATA)
Headquarters
One Motngomery Street
Telesis Tower
Suite 1000
San Francisco, CA 941-4-4539
USA

Pacific Asia Travel Association (PATA)
Pacific Division
GPO Box 645
Kings Cross NSW 2283
 Telephone: (02) 9332 3599
 Facsimile: (02) 9331 6592

The Ecotourism Society
PO Box 755
North Bennington
VT 05257-0755
USA
 Telephone: 0011 1 802 447 2121
 Facsimile: 0011 1 802 447 2122

New Zealand

New Zealand Tourism Indutry Association
PO Box 1697
Wellington
New Zealand
 Telephone:(04) 499 0104
 Facsimile: (04) 499 0827

Inbounc Tourism Organisations
Council of New Zealand (ITOC)
PO Box 1888
Wellington
New Zealand
    Telephone:(04) 384 2063
    Facsimile: (04) 385 8091

KiwiHost
New Zealand Tourism Board
PO Box 95
Wellington
New Zealand
    Telephone:(04) 472 8860
    Facsimile: (04) 478 1736

New Zealand Association of Farm
and Home Hosts Inc
PO Box 56
Auckland
New Zealand
    Telephone:(09) 810 9175
    Facsimile: (09) 810 9448

NZ Natural Heritage Foundation
Massey University
Palmerston North
New Zealand
    Telephone:(06) 356 9099
    Facsimile: (06) 356 7286

Heritage Trails Foundation
PO Box 3273
Christchruch
New Zealand
    Telephone:(03) 365 2769
    Facsimile: (03) 365 2698

New Zealand Adventure Tourism
Council
PO Box 1697
Wellington
New Zealand

Qualmark New Zealand Ltd
PO Box 1488
Auckland
New Zealand
    Facsimile: (09) 377 2132

New Zealand Automobile Association
Inc
PO Box 5
Auckalnd
New Zealand
    Facsimile: (09) 309 4564

Australia

Ecotourism Association of Australia
(EAA)
GPO Box 1122
Brisbane QLD 4001
    Telephone: (07) 3221 1811
    Facsmilie: (07) 3221 3270

Tourism Council Australia (TCA)
PO Box E328
Queen Victoria Terrace
Barton ACT 2600
    Telephone: (02) 6273 1000
    Facsimile: (02) 6273 4999

Inbound Tourism Organisation of
Australia (ITOA)
GPO Box 646
Kings Cross NSW 2011
    Telephone: (02) 9360 5955
    Facsimile: (02) 9332 3383

AussieHost
Level 2
80 William Street
Woolloomooloo NSW 2011
    Telephone: (02) 9332 3416
    Facsimile: (02) 9332 3383

Australian Farm and Country Tourism
Inc (AFACT)
6th Floor
230 Collins Street
Melbourne VIC 3000
Telephone: (03) 9650 2922
Facsimile: (03) 9650 9434

Australian Bed and Breakfast Council
Blind Creek
RMB 4110
Benalla VIC 3672
Telephone: (03) 5762 2792
Facsimile: (03) 5762 4078

Australian Automobile Association (AAA)
GPO Box 155
Canberra ACT 2601
Telephone: (02) 6247 7311
Facsimile: (02) 6257 5320

Outdoor Recreation Council of
Australia (ORCA)
PO Box 422
North Sydney NSW 2059
Telephone: (02) 9923 4275
Facsimile: (02) 9923 4237

Australian State Tourism Bodies

New South Wales Tourism
Commission
GPO Box 7050
Sydney NSW 2001
Telephone: (02) 9931 1464
Facsimile: (02) 9931 1424

Tourism Victoria
GPO Box 2219T
Melbourne Vic 3001
Telephone: (03) 9653 9777
Facsimile: (03) 9653 9744

Queensland Travel & Tourism
Corporation
GPO Box 328
Brisband QLD 4001
Telephone: (07) 3833 5400
Facsimile: (07) 3833 5487

Western Australian Tourism
Commission
16 St. Georges Terrace, Perth
Western Australia, 6000
Telephone: (08) 9220 1700
Facsimile: (08) 9220 1702

Department of Tourism, Sport and
Recreation (Tas)
GPO Box 399
Hobart Tas 7001
Telephone: (03) 6233 8011
Facsimile: (03) 3620 8353

South Australian Tourism
Commission
GPO Box 1972
Terrace Towers
78 North Terrace
Adelaide 5001 South Australia
Telephone: (08) 8303 2222
Facsimilie: (08) 8303 2295

Northern Territory Tourist
Commission
PO Box 1155
Darwin NT 0801
Telephone: (08) 8999 3900
Facsimile: (08) 8999 3888

ACT Tourism Commission
GPO Box 744
Canberra ACT 2601
Freecall: 1800 026 166
Telephone: (02) 6205 0044
Facsimile: (02) 6205 0776.

Indigenous Communities and Tourism

The following contacts can provide more information about becoming involved in indigenous tourism.

New Zealand

Aoteroa Maori Tourism Federation (Inc)
PO Box 34
Rotorua
New Zealand

Te Puni Kokiri – Ministry of Maori Development
Massey House
PO Box 3949
Wellington
New Zealand
Telephone:(04) 499 0055
Facsimile: (04) 495 0831

Australia

Nature-based and Indigenous Tourism Regional Development Branch
Department of Industry, Science and Tourism
GPO Box 1545
Canberra ACT 2601
Telephone:(03) 6279 7126
Facsimile: (03) 6279 7189

National Aboriginal and Torres Strait Islander Tourism Strategy (NATSITS)
ATSIC
PO Box 17
Woden ACT 2606
Telephone: (03) 6289 8881
Facsimile: (03) 6282 5027

Private Sector Strategies Section
Aboriginal Employment Strategies Branch
Department of Employment, Education and Training
GPO Box 9880
Canberra ACT 2601
Telephone: (03) 6276 8980
Facsimile: (03) 6276 8970

Conservation and Environment

World Wide Fund for Nature International (WFF)
World Conservation Centre
Avenue du Mont Blanc
1196 Gland
Switzerland
Telephone: 0011 4122 364 9111
Facsimile: 0011 4122 364 5829

World Wide Fund for Nature (WFF)
Australia
Level 1, 71 York Street
Sydney NSW 2000, Australia
Telephone: 61-2-92996366
Fax: 61-2-92996656

Green Globe
World Travel and Tourism Council
4 Suffolk Place
London
SW1Y 4BS
United Kingdom
Telephone: 0011 44 71 222 1955
Facsimile: 0011 44 71 223 890285

New Zealand

Ministry for the Environment (Manatu
Mo Te Taiao)
PO Box 10362
84 Boulcott St
Wellington
New Zealand
    Telephone: (04) 917 7400
    Facsimile: (04) 917 7523

Department of Conservation (Te Papa
Atawhai)
Boulcott Street
PO Box 10-420
Wellington
New Zealand
    Telephone: (04) 471-0726.

Landcare Research,
PO Box 40,
Lincoln
New Zealand
    Telephone: (03) 325 6700
    Facsimile: (03) 325 2127

Australia

Department of the Environment
GPO Box 787
15 Moore Street
Canberra ACT 2601
    Telephone: (02) 6274 1111
    Facsimile: (02) 6274 1123

National Landcare Program
Land and Water Resources Division
Department of Primary Industries and
Energy
GPO Box 858
CANBERRA ACT 2601
    Telephone: (02) 6271 6610
    Facsimile: (02) 6272 5618

Greening Austalia Limited
GPO Box 9868
Canberra ACT 2601
    Telephone: (03) 6281 8585
    Facsimile: (03) 6281 8590

Energy and Waste Minimisation

New Zealand

Energy Efficiency and Conservation
Authority (EECA)
22 The Terrace
PO Box 388
Wellington
New Zealand
    Telephone: (04) 470 2200
    Facsimile: (04) 499 5330

1st Floor, 177 Parnell Road
PO Box 37-444
Parnell
Auckland
    Telephone: (09) 377 5328
    Facsimile: (09) 366 0531

Unit B, 52 Mandeville St
PO Box 8562
Riccarton
Christchurch
    Telephone: (03) 341 1126
    Facsimile: (03) 343 1219

Australia

Environment Protection Agency
40 Blackall Street
Barton ACT 2600
    Telephone: (06) 274 1999
    Toll Free: 008 803 772
    Facsimile: (06) 274 1666

Enterprise Energy Audit Program
Industry and Government Section
Energy Programs and Fisheries
Division
Department of Primary Industries and
Energy
GPO Box 858
Canberra ACT 2601
    Telephone: (06) 272 4763
    Facsimile: (06) 273 1232

Enterprise Improvement Services
AusIndustry
51 Allara Street
Canberra ACT 2601
    Telephone: (06) 276 1655
    Facsimile: (06) 276 1586

Industry Bodies

Australian Solid Fuel and Wood
Heating Association
7 South Road
Brighton VIC 3186
    Telephone: (03) 9592 2522
    Facsimile: (03) 9592 8080

Environment Management Industry
Association of Australia
Unit 1, Level 6
Anzac Square Building
202 Adelaide Street
PO Box 2231
Brisbane QLD 4000
    Telephone: (07) 3229 8522
    Facsimile: (07) 3229 8577

Plastics and Chemicals Industry
Association
4th Floor
380 St Kilda Road
GPO Box 16010M
Melbourne VIC 3004
    Telephone: (03) 9699 6299
    Facsimile: (03) 9699 6717

Solar Energy Industries Association of
Australia
1st Floor
505 St Kilda Road
Melbourne VIC 3004
    Telephone: (03) 9866 8977
    Facsimile: (03) 9866 8922

Sustainable Energy Industries Council
of Australia
    PO Box 411
    Dickson ACT 2602
    Telephone: (03) 6241 9260
    Facsimile: (03) 6241 9266

Alternative Technology Association
247 Flinders Lane
Melbourne VIC 3000
    Telephone: (03) 9650 7883
    Facsimile: (03) 9650 8574

Australian Institute of Energy
PO Box 230
Wahroonga NSW 2076
    Telephone: (02) 9449 1800

Ecodesign Foundation Inc
PO Box 369
Rozelle NSW 2039
    Telephone: (02) 9555 9412
    Facsimile: (02) 9555 9564

Waste Management Association of
Australia
PO Box 146
Chatswood NSW 2057
　　Telephone: (02) 9281 7655
　　Facsimile: (02) 9313 8442

Volunteer Environmental Tourism Groups

Willing Workers on Organic Farms
(WOOF)
Po Box 10 037
Palmerston North
New Zealand
　　Telephone:(06) 355 3555

Australian Trust for Conservation
Volunteers
PO Box 423
Ballarat VIC 3350
　　Telephone: (053) 32 7490
　　Facsimile: (053) 332290

Earthwatch
457 Elisabeth Street
Melbourne VIC 3000
　　Telephone: (03) 9600 9100
　　Facsimile: (03) 9600 9066

Australian and New Zealand Scientific
Exploration Society
PO Box 174
Albert Park VIC 3206
　　Telephone: (03) 9690 5455
　　Facsimile: (03) 9690 0151

Regional tourism associations and development organisations are also useful contacts. Local government authorities can usually provide contact information for the relevant bodies.